A

Book

of

Revelations

A

Book

of

Revelations

**Lesbian and Gay Episcopalians
Tell Their Own Stories**

Edited by Louie Crew
Associate Professor, Rutgers University

With a Foreword by George N. Hunt
The Bishop of Rhode Island

Integrity, Inc.

1991

FIRST EDITION

Cover Design: Gina Moss
Production Coordination: Edgar Kim Byham

Library of Congress Cataloging-in-Publication Data

Crew, Louie, 1936-
    A book of revelations.

Catalog Card Number: 91-133978
ISBN: 0-9629506-0-2

Integrity, Inc. is the Lesbian and Gay Justice Ministry of the Episcopal Church, with chapters throughout the United States and affiliated chapters in Canada and Australia. Since 1974, Integrity's goal has been to both bring the lesbian and gay community fully into the Episcopal Church and to bring the Episcopal Church fully into the lesbian and gay community. We welcome memberships from non-lesbian/gay persons and from non-Episcopalians. Members receive a quarterly publication, *The Voice of Integrity*.

JOIN INTEGRITY!

_____Individual $25.00

_____Couple $40.00

_____Student/Senior Citizen $10.00

Send with check or money order to:
Integrity, Inc., P.O. Box 19561, Washington, DC 20036-0561.
For Information about Integrity, call 718-720-3054.

FOREWORD

In 1988 the Standing Commission on Human Affairs and Health of the Episcopal Church, which I chaired, asked our Church

> to suspend -- just for the moment -- the ancient judgments against our present homosexual Episcopalians and simply allow them to tell the stories of their lives. When did they realize or fear that they were homosexuals? What was the reaction of their parents? The reaction of their church? What is the price they have paid? What are their hopes within the Church? We realize this is an ambitious and, perhaps, threatening task. But it can be done, and if it were, the Body of Christ would be far less estranged. The cry for justice would begin to be heard. It is not a matter of "coming out of the closet" or "staying in" but a matter of finding another room where we can talk. That room must be found.

We went on to say: "We do not think that homosexual Episcopalians need or deserve another rejection at this moment. Instead, this moment cries out for us to find a non-judgmental occasion to listen and talk and to lay aside, for a while, our chronic adversarial posturing."

The 1988 General Convention of the Episcopal Church responded with a resolution stating, in part,

> That this Convention, responsive to the call of the Standing Commission on Human Affairs and Health "to find a non-judgmental occasion to listen and talk," and in the spirit of the Presiding Bishop's statement that "there will be no outcasts in this Church," strongly urge

each diocese and congregation to provide opportunities for open dialogue on human sexuality, in which we, as members of this Church, both heterosexual and homosexual, may study, pray, listen to, and share our convictions and concerns, our search for stable, loving and committed relationships, and our journey toward wholeness and holiness...

Unfortunately, over the past three years, the adversarial posturing has not abated; indeed it has intensified in some arenas. Yet, the ambitious program of listening to and sharing the concerns of the lesbians and gay men in the Episcopal Church has begun, although on a rather slow and timorous basis.

Only thirty-three of the ninety-nine domestic dioceses of the Episcopal Church sent in responses to our questionnaires. While not all of those have initiated dialogue, half of those responding reported positive results from engaging in dialogue. The now renamed Commission on Human Affairs not surprisingly concluded in our 1991 Report to General Convention, "One immediate finding was that much of the church is reluctant to engage in open dialogue on human sexuality."

Because we are so reluctant to speak with one another, I welcome the opportunity that Integrity is giving us in this book. Our Commission held open hearings around the country for three years, and I had an opportunity to hear and share the pain of lesbian and gay Episcopalians. Now *A Book of Revelations* gives everyone else in the church an opportunity to hear many of those same stories. I hope everyone will take advantage of this opportunity.

The Rt. Rev. George N. Hunt
Bishop of Rhode Island

INTRODUCTION

"Argument provides argument, reason is met by sophistry. But narratives...go right to the heart," said an 1849 reviewer whom Henry Louis Gates, Jr. cites in *The Classic Slave Narratives* (Mentor, 1987, page xii).

In *A Book of Revelations* fifty-two lesbians and gay men narrate their journeys for you to ponder in the privacy of your heart. As in earlier catacombs, most narrators share only a Christian name. Ten work in education -- two as teachers, four as professors, three as students, one as an administrator of a teachers' union. Three work in publishing -- one as a writer, another as an editor, another as an administrative assistant for a law review. Three work in the business sector. One is a hairdresser. Three work in public health -- one as a medical doctor, another as psychologist, and another as a staff person for the V.A. Eight are priests.

Others have not mentioned their vocations. Some are in *Who's Who*, but have chosen not to say so. The narrators focus not on what they do, but on who they are and who God is. They celebrate faith not celebrity, justice not sex, hope not comfort, love not retribution.

Episcopal leaders send us contrary messages about lesbian and gay people. A few warn us that these are dangerous outsiders and that we should not ordain anyone who even advocates treating lesbians and gays as one of us. Others ask us to reverse traditional prejudice, to cast out no one, to call unclean no one whom God has made. A great many others invite us to ignore lesbians and gays as much as possible, to treat them as persons not mentionable among Anglicans in good standing.

This cacophony goes a long way towards explaining why fewer than one percent of all congregations have issued invitations for lesbians and gays tell our stories, though General Convention urged all to do so. The congregations of deputies alone could have increased the response several hundred percent.

The Episcopal Church does not often unabashedly give out bad checks. Why in this case has it boldly said one thing and flagrantly done the opposite? Why have bishops and deputies invested no capital, spiritual or material, to keep their check from bouncing? For example, in the last three years not one bishop has invited an openly lesbian or gay male to speak at a diocesan convention. Not one has taken along an openly lesbian or gay male chaplain to parish visitations. The few bishops who have dared publicly to affirm lesbians and gays faced steady calumny and other abuse.

Dioceses have also balked. Only a mere seventeen percent of the domestic dioceses reported any dialogue at all, and most of that discussion took place only in closed quarters with special task forces or committees -- a far cry from the "congregations" specified by General Convention. Nor has the Episcopal Church Center prepared any mechanism to facilitate dialogue.

A Book of Revelations documents the neglect and the malice which lesbians and gays face again and again in the Episcopal Church. Some have been excommunicated. Others have been driven to heterosexual experience with disastrous consequences for their spouses, their children, and other family members. Many have lost their jobs and been driven from their homes. One is in prison.

These are not the voices of those who leave the Church, but of those who stay, in spite of the fierce caprice. We stay not at the Church's invitation, but at God's.

God is faithful and hears the cries of the oppressed. It would be disastrous for any lesbian or gay to knock saying, "Let me in." Lesbians and gays already are *in*, already are loved fully and unconditionally by God, already *are* the Church, already are privileged to suffer for the Faith, as these narratives reveal. We need your help in sharing this Good News.

Louie Crew
Newark
Easter, 1991

Blessed are you, when you suffer insults and persecution and calumnies of every kind for my sake. Exult and be glad, for you have a rich reward in heaven; in the same way they persecuted the prophets before you. You are the salt of the world.

Matthew 5:11-13

Contents

Mabelle's Story

Recently, at the elementary school where I teach, I indulged in a little nostalgia by re-reading the children's book *The Emperor's New Clothes.* Remember it? A king walks naked among his subjects showing off his "new" clothes. His subjects act like they see his new clothes and even compliment him on them. Finally, a young boy says, "The king has on no clothes!" Rather than behave properly, the boy simply spoke out when what he saw and what he heard did not jibe!

The story brought to mind my feelings most any Sunday at my Episcopal parish. We pass the peace as if all is well. Is it? Not with me.

My parish has a large number of gay and lesbian members. Everyone knows that lesbian and gay members are accepted. Yes, there is far more acceptance here than at my previous fundamentalist churches, and for that I am grateful. But I expect more. Mere acceptance requires no action. In these days of discrimination against gay and lesbian people--discrimination in areas of sexual law, jobs, insurance, tax benefits, inheritance, adoptions, etc.--we need the church to do something, not merely "accept" us. What is the church doing about gay bashings, about the horror that goes along with AIDS, or about the blessing of committed lesbian and gay relationships? What is the church doing to make common everyday things that heterosexuals take for granted at my parish--like holding hands with your spouse, giving your spouse a peck on the cheek, having your anniversary recognized during the Prayers of the People--a reality for its gay and lesbian members also? Lesbians and gays would be accused of flaunting their sexuality if they acted in these "normal" ways. Mere acceptance rings hollow.

I see people who act as if the king has new clothes, as if all is well in the kingdom. Others in the pews tell me that the "establishment" prefers not to "spotlight" a particular group in the congregation, but instead prefers that we work to integrate into the whole. I'm all for integration--but we must address the problems first. In the 60s, the Episcopal church, and especially my parish, spoke out--from the pulpit, in the newsletter, at church school classes, and probably even during social gatherings--against racial discrimination. Today, can't it speak out against homophobia? Can't it affirm the lesbians and gay males already inside the Episcopal Church?

I try not to be a single-issue person in my Christianity or in my politics. But I think no one in my present parish understands how this single issue affects me on a daily basis. So right now, I'm searching for a parish that has at least a few members with the honest spirit of the little boy from *The Emperor's New Clothes*. I hope they will be among the clergy and in the congregation. They will know what they see is not right and will say something about it. With their support and their strength behind me, I will finally be able to pass the peace with peace in my heart.

Josh's Story

N. wilt thou have this Man to thy wedded husband, to live together after God's ordinance in the holy estate of Matrimony? Wilt thou love him, comfort him, honor, and keep him in sickness and in health; and, forsaking all others, keep thee only unto him, so long as ye both shall live?

--The Book of Common Prayer (1928)

That's what "marriage" was like when I was growing up. As an acolyte, I served at dozens of weddings; and the Episcopal Church's use of language and symbol, "promulgating the truths of the Gospel to mankind in the clearest, plainest, most affecting and majestic manner," always moved me.

Years later, when I met a man so good, so solid that getting married seemed nearly possible for us as gay men, we often talked and half-planned what our wedding would be like. Naturally, I wanted the finest church wedding imaginable. We would enter the nave from separate corners in the back of the church, then meet and walk together down the center aisle. That would liturgize our separateness as individuals, our unity as a couple. And he would be on my left; somehow, I felt the taller man should be on the left.

And while I heartily approve of them for others, I did not want a "Holy Union" in a gay church, or a surreptitious service at home with a priest acting without the bishop's knowledge or approval. We would hold out for that approval and not give them the satisfaction of making us say our vows in the closet. Even if we had to wait for years, I said, we would one day have a public wedding, in the church, with the string quartet and the gold rings and the priest's stole wrapped around our joined hand as we knelt at the altar of God.

And the priest would read the liturgy like Father Ben used to do. And the mass would be shatteringly beautiful, the faithful would weep and a hundred gay men in the congregation would sing us all into heaven. And Mike Leamon would play the piano at our reception, at the Netherland Hotel, the gay social event of the years--and every other flight of fancy imaginable.

But "life is what happens to you while you're planning for something else."

Jack got sick.

And the Church debated, but approval did not come.

One night in the hospital, after all the operations and the pain and the fear, I asked Jack to think about what kind of tuxedo he wanted to wear at our wedding. Life was suddenly fragile, and we needed something to hope for and look forward to. We never set a date, but holding out for the ideal circumstances seemed less important than loving each other right now.

And when we did get married, whether in his wheelchair or with his artificial legs, Jack would still be on the left. The taller man belongs on the left.

Sick for a year. Then in the hospital and four operations. Out for five days, then back in and another amputation. Out for three weeks at Christmas--three

4

whole weeks--and we laughed as well as cried. Then back in again, and another amputation.

And I began to realize that I did not want to be a care-giver for the rest of my life. Carting around wheel-chairs, running after prescriptions and those damn dressings that no store carries, all of the banking and shopping and the post office, then home for the cooking and cleaning and comforting and motivating and laun-dering and shampooing: "I didn't sign on for all this!"

And an echo said.

I *N.* take thee N. to be my wedded Husband, to have and to hold from this day forward, for better for worse, for richer for poorer, in sickness and in health, to love and to cherish, till death us do part, according to God's holy ordinance; and thereto I give thee my troth.

So along with the anger and frustration and worry and grieving, just what I needed: guilt!

Not that I ever seriously considered leaving him. How could I? He's so much fun--still, now more than ever! He's so right for me.

But for once I could understand, finally, what some friends had said to me early on in Jack's hospitalization: "I admire you for staying with him. Somebody else might have left." The first time I heard that, I was shocked.

Of course we know abandonment happens, especially to people with AIDS; but I'd always despised such fair weather lovers. How could they do that, punish someone they supposedly loved, as soon as he got sick? On top of everything else he has to endure, Jerry Falwell to Ryan White, food trays left outside his door, rejection from parents, the disease of the century, the horror and suffering and pain--abandon your lover because he got AIDS, disgusting! Guys who do that should be shot!

Well, I am new at this caregiver role, desperately proud of what I've been able to do, but always an inch from falling off the edge.

I don't give advice to you, caregivers; I'm not qualified; but I am learning something: it's all right to let yourself feel like you want to run away. If you don't have permission to consider that possibility, you're not really making the choice to stay.

And your lover will know that somehow, sense the dishonesty of it, realize that you're resentful and ill-used and martyring yourself so that you can oppress him with your righteousness. And there he is, needy and fearful, not having the freedom to leave you--making him resentful, ill-used, and sick on top of it. For who will take care of him if he throws you out the door?

Wilt thou have this Man to thy wedded husband, to live together after God's ordinance in the holy estate of Matrimony? Wilt thou love him, comfort him, honor, and keep him in sickness and in health; and forsaking all others, keep thee only unto him, so long as ye both shall live?

The Woman shall answer,

I will.

6

I will, Jack; I think I will. That's probably the best thing I could do for myself.

I wouldn't trade your warmth and wit for anything else I can think of today. Tomorrow will take care of itself, of course; it always does. And I wouldn't be surprised if I make the same choice tomorrow; for how else could I keep such a promise, "forsaking all others, keeping me only unto you, so long as we both shall live," than in the now, and for today?

Besides, as Martha said, this craziness I'm going through tonight is probably that I'm mourning your right foot. That just happened a couple days ago, and I haven't got used to it yet emotionally; and things are different now, it's another big change. We were both depending on that right foot...

But it sure was fun seeing you tonight, out of the gown and into your "dress sweats" and out of bed. It sure was fun massaging your shoulders in the elevator, wheeling down for chocolate soft-serve in the cafeteria.

See you tomorrow, babe. You're my guy.

Will's Story

Even at six or seven, I set out on a path which would lead both to the Church and to gay sexuality. I'm not sure which truth about me would make my father more uncomfortable.

My father held violent prejudices against Jews, blacks, women, gays, and Catholics. I deem homophobic prejudice to be as unacceptable in our society as those other prejudices which in recent years we have begun to clear away. His example persuaded me that all prejudice springs from a single source, whatever its object of scorn.

My parents raised me with no religion. My father had lapsed as a Baptist, and my mother had lapsed as a Christian Scientist. Nevertheless, I held a strong belief in God, and in the reality of the world of the spirit. As a child, I constructed my own religion out of bits and pieces of observed ritual and belief. Almost at the same time there came the first manifestations of attraction to men, sexual only in the vague way of pre-adolescent fascination, but clearly physical, attached to images of men at the beach, or heroes in the movies. To what extent did both impulses, the religious and the sexual, arise out of the same psychic needs? Did they connect to my father? Even then our relationship progressively disintegrated, in part due to problems of his which I had no way of comprehending.

I experienced slow, often painful growth, a mixture of struggle and grace, toward the ability to love, as prescribed in those two commandments given us by Christ, to love God and to love our fellow man. I know, of course, that God didn't have in mind erotic love, though

I'm not so sure that God totally excluded it either. Like many gay men and women, I am heartened by the research of scholars like John Boswell, which seems to indicate that the Church has not always been so hostile to same-sex relationships as some would have us believe. Surely, too, I am heartened by our church's capacity to grow to new understandings of the Gospel, making room for women to play roles in the Church that might have shocked St. Paul. Not too many years ago, pious Christians found scriptural support for the institution of slavery, and in our own century biblical support has been cited for segregation. Perhaps because I came to the Church later in life and with a good knowledge of history, I see it as a growing, evolving, organic body, responding to new challenges with new understanding of the Scriptures.

My model of a growing Church is grounded partly in history, but perhaps even more in my own personal story. Inevitably, I did not remain at the childish stage of celebrating funerals for my pets and fantasizing about the luminous masculine figures in the movies. Adolescence brought both religious crisis and sexual crisis, and I reacted to both by repressing them. My personal religion became secretive and exclusive, as did my sexual life. Adopting the prejudices of my father and society at large, I was convinced that my sexual feelings were wicked and that they needed to be stamped out.

I felt absolutely no desire, nor did I have the capacity, to enter into the heterosexual mating games of my peers. I felt deeply estranged, and was drawn to other boys and girls who shared this estrangement. We were all outsiders, not really knowing why.

9

In recent years I have re-established contact with this little band of friends from junior high school days, only to discover that four of my closest male friends from that time have turned out to be gay. Two didn't discover that fact until long after they had married and had children. Their coming to terms with their sexuality was wrenching for them and their families, but the alternative was to live in what had become for them a continuous lie, undermining the integrity of what should have been the central commitment of their lives.

My own sense of isolation protected me from making this mistake, but at the cost of keeping me afraid to be honest with anyone. It was a life virtually devoid of love - how can love exist without openness or honesty? It lasted until I was in graduate school, at Princeton University. I had spent a year in Europe before going there, and I had been drawn to the services at the Roman Catholic cathedral in Freiburg, Germany, where I was studying. I must have become something of a crypto-Catholic, but without any inclination to cross the barrier of exclusion that existed in my religious life as well as in my emotional life. I could love neither God nor my fellow man.

It was at Princeton that two great breakthroughs took place. While the sexual guilt kept me from exploring the gay life that was available there, I did develop for the first time an openness to friendship: intense, emotional, full of thwarted sexual longings, but real friendships as I had never known before.

In my last year of graduate study, one of these friends found his way to the services of the Episcopal chaplaincy at Princeton, led by Father Ronald Cox, a wonderful man who possessed the great gifts of understanding and compassion that made it possible for him to accept my narration of who and what I was. He affirmed and guided me.

His message went something like this: I believe that God intends for men and women to be drawn to each other, and that you should search in yourself for the possibility of this way of loving. But ultimately what matters is love itself. It is better to love someone, to be able to love whoever it may be, than to close yourself off from love entirely. Some might think he should have insisted that I might love, but never express it sexually. That was not what he said. Perhaps he was so happy and fulfilled in his own marriage that he could not imagine imposing lifelong celibacy on a young man in whom he saw the first glimmerings of long-repressed warmth and love.

So it was that within a short time, I found the beginnings of my relationship with God, was baptized and confirmed in the Episcopal Church, and received permission, as it were, to begin to realize my sexuality. That same spring I came out. The coming out, I must admit, had very little of love about it. It was largely a matter of pure lust, and I felt a mixture of relief, freedom, and shame. I was a neophyte in the Church, and a sexual neophyte as well. The pattern was beginning to take shape.

In an odd, some might say, perverse way, the two capacities for love would grow throughout the succeeding years, so that I come to the present moment feeling that I could not be a Christian had I not come to terms with my gayness, were I not convinced that God's love embraces me as I am, and that my love for another man is grounded in the source of all love. Nor could I have

11

come to a fulfilled, loving relationship with another man if I were not grounded in a vital spirituality.

Over the years I have grown spiritually, both through the Church and through my own life experiences. I have grown, too, in my capacity for love, in my discernment of what love is. Not only because of the threat of AIDS or because of the diminished energy of middle age, I have come to appreciate what it means to have a stable, committed, loving relationship. My relationship, too, has grown over a fifteen-year period. It began in passion and romance, but from the beginning I knew that this man, Charles, was a very special man. More than once I have told him that most of what I know about love I have learned from him. He has taken me to a new understanding of devotion, commitment, forgiveness, and affirmation. There have been some rough times, and I have had to come to terms with the fact that this isn't the all-fulfilling relationship that we all fantasized about in our youth.

I know, too, that there have been some rough times in my relationship with the Church. I have not always found there the fulfillment that I expected, and I have grieved at the factionalism and especially at the love-lessness that manifests itself at times. I grieve, too, that so many in the Church are unable to accept that God could manifest His love in my life through this relationship that is to me what marriage and family are to others.

I know that I could leave this Church and turn, for example, to the Metropolitan Community Church, as have many of my friends. But I have no intention of doing that. I believe that this is the true body of Christ, and that like all bodies, like every living thing created by God, it is growing and becoming more perfectly what it is meant to be.

I believe that, as it has grown to accept new roles for women in the Church, it is possible that our Church will grow also to a new understanding of human sexuality, and recognize, to quote the chant, *ubi caritas et amor, Deus ibi est.* Where there is charity and love, there also is God.

For reasons unknowable to me, the capacity to love, which in most people links to sexual desire for persons of the opposite sex, linked for me to desire for persons of my same sex. But the love is the same, the desire the same, and, I believe, is the same gift of God. As once the Church had to come to realize that the food which had once been called unclean could now be called clean, that Gentiles who had once been called unclean could now share a meal with Jews who had spent their lives keeping the Law, so I have hope that in our own time the embrace of the Church will widen once again. Here, too, in my life and the lives of my friends, God is present.

Jay's Story

I watched a glorious sunset at age 4, my first moment of ecstasy, indelible and unequaled in my memory. As poignantly, I remember how, at age 7, my friend Charles ran across the meadow and embraced and kissed me. We both blushed and felt good.

At school I was an "outsider," but I was fortunate in that I could smugly attribute this to jealousy. I was always the class "genius" and teacher's pet -- except in gym.

Jim and I were lead sopranos in the church choir, sat together, and passed time during the sermon playing with each other's fingers--another indelible memory of ecstasy. Our voices changed and he moved away to end up later, I learned, a choirmaster and organist out west.

My life became complicated. Spontaneous erections. Naughty thoughts. Soon I learned that I could rid myself of these thoughts with a little handshake, especially if I kept my mind busy and my fingers otherwise occupied as much as possible. Girls and the social whirl did not bother me too much, since I was popular as the organizer and operator of functions which left my "date" free, usually to her relief as well as mine.

With a boy it was different, because whenever I would inadvertently reach out with a natural gesture, he would withdraw -- and more strangely, when he reached out I would sense warmth which he would instantly replace with alarm verging on terror. Our private school once banished one friend, with no explanation.

In graduate school and the army, others "disappeared" for "suspicion" of acts unspecified.

I joined the medical faculty and became part of the "establishment." Once I sat on a "personnel evaluation" panel. When "the subject" came up I said nothing. Another time, I believe I might have saved a young resident physician from suicide if I had only said something. But I had become a victim of homophobia.

In high school I cavorted with a group of Irish Roman Catholic boys for whom drinking and having fun was a proper healthy "sin." In due course they took me to an establishment where I undertook an experiment which I found clinical but emotionally distasteful. The young woman impressed me with her kind attitude and her professionalism, and I have retained a benevolent attitude toward these professionals whose services I spurn.

I survived schooling and went to war. During my internship I met a nurse on 3 North working on her master's degree at the University and taking scholastic philosophy as an elective. We spent evenings together, when the floor was quiet, discussing Aquinas and like matters. We seemed to have many common interests. Only years later could I realize or admit that we had gayness in common as well, and that the greatest attraction must have been the implication of heterosexual demands.

Returning from the war, I knew that I had reached the age when marriage was mandated -- no options, such was my acculturation. So with great courage I came to visit this young woman, proposed marriage, received the Anglican rites in a private ceremony, and returned home to start practice, while she as Director of Nursing completed her contract with the hospital back east.

Once together we took our marital obligations very seriously, following the rules laid out in our medical and psychology textbooks for the successful marriage. We spaced three children properly, and sent them to proper schools. We saw to their spiritual development and become pillars of the church. I was busy with the practice and in teaching young residents. She was active in the church and with other ladies' groups. We dated each other regularly, going out to the opera, the club, the theater, private parties, civic functions. We had sex two or three times weekly as prescribed in the scientific literature, and one could fall back on youthful practices when tension became too demanding.

All went well until doing prescribed duties eventually led to "burnout" and change-of-life drew nigh. Looking back, I was using the patients and the bright young residents to keep me, to use Freud's term, sublimated. But God was not so naughty as to lead me so far into temptation as to fracture our fiction.

My wife and co-conspirator did not approve of any drugs or tobacco and hardly of aspirin. Too late I realized she excluded beverage alcohol. Alcohol became the means for her to ease the conflict between what the church had taught her and what she truly felt sexually. Death pursued her inexorably.

I missed her deeply, left alone in depression and confusion. The children were at college. A neighbor widow kindly offered a relationship, but repulsed me. The church substituted pious platitudes for genuine help. Was my plight even relevant to Christ? The church teachings had spiritually entrapped my wife, as she went from Eddyism through Romanism into Anglicanism. This entrapment led to her addiction and death.

About this time science revealed evidence that sexual orientation is inborn and genetically determined in the human and other mammals. No longer could notions of sin or disease support the church's homophobia. Orientation is a biological given -- in religious terms, the will of God, under God's control alone. Contrary scriptural "interpretations" become indefensible. Then AIDS appeared. I met PWA's in my medical practice. The "gay problem" was obviously society's problem.

When it denies and rejects any consideration of God's intentions for the gay segment of baptized Christians, the Church leaves this group adrift without relevant moral guidance. When the Church refuses to consider sex as a spiritual force, it behaves destructively both to itself and to the faithful. The latter have the option of walking away. The Church will continue to lose, to the point of suicide, if it remains obstinate.

The Church has been ignored on divorce, on contraception, on premarital exploration and post-marital friendship, but will not admit it. The Church has dealt with gayness through hypocrisy.

Celibacy promotes cancer of both prostate and spirit, and lacks explicit scriptural sanction. Morality based on ignorance and error opposes God and natural law; it cannot endure.

A cradle Episcopalian, I know that I have, with my background in Christianity, medicine, and teaching received a special call from God to help my Church in this crisis.

Jean's Story

I want the Church to bless my relationship. My partner and I have been committed to each other for 4 years. Since the time of our commitment, life has not been easy, because of homophobia and outside pressures. We have overcome many adversities to be together. We think our relationship is worth this work.

As a committed lesbian couple, we sincerely desire "marriage," even more sincerely than many heterosexual couples. We have committed ourselves to each other, monogamously. We want the Church to bless our commitment and to celebrate with us. We need the Church's support and strength when the times get tough.

Some wonder why many homosexuals do not stay together long. Why should that surprise? Who supports them? No one!

Society defines for gay relationships no definite starting place--no marriage, no divorce. When two people become identified as a couple on a specific date, they feel greater responsibility for the commitment they claim to make.

When gay people end a relationship, they have no legal responsibility. They have no legal responsibility for each other.

The Church provides little extra support. Yes, the priest greets you at the door, pats you both on the back, and asks how things are going; but when the parish announces a new "couples Bible study," the parish does not expect my partner and me to show up. Perhaps they should call it the "heterosexual couples' Bible study."

Does the Church recognize our anniversary? No.

Is our anniversary important to them? No.

Does the priest lay hands on us to bless and celebrate our 10th year together? No.

How hard will the church make it for us to stay together? Many church people actually encourage couples to break up. When my spouse and I have problems, can we go to a priest or a bishop for counseling? Can I?

Homosexuality will not go away.

I love my church. I love God. I hope that someday the church will recognize my partner and me for the love we share. The happiness which our relationship brings to us deserves sharing, with the whole state of Christ's church.

Frank's Story

I became attracted to my sixth grade teacher in a way I didn't understand; he was unaware of it. During junior high school and high school I had crushes on other boys; they were always unaware of it.

I read in a book on child development that children are first interested in their own gender but, as they mature, they gradually become interested in the opposite gender instead. Thus, I assumed that my feelings were simply a result of immaturity and that they would go away as I aged.

But, the feelings unnerved me. When near an attractive boy, I would become nervous, tongue-tied, and weak-kneed.

In my third year of college, I temporarily dropped out, in December 1958, because of academic problems. At the time, I was involved in a relationship with someone who was irresponsible, uncommitted, only sporadically supportive, and totally inappropriate for me. However, because of extreme feelings of isolation and a total lack of self-confidence, I was highly dependent on him and unable to break the relationship. I hurt.

To get to the root of my academic problems, my father had me see a psychiatrist. After several interviews, I told him that I was gay. During a subsequent interview, he obtained permission to tell my parents by falsely stating that they suspected. My parents, who lived out of town, drove to Saint Paul to see him, then drove to my boarding house in Minneapolis to see me. What followed was by far the most traumatic experience in my life.

My father had me get into the car to talk. The way I was treated was so bad that I can't begin to think of adequate words to describe it. For all practical purposes, I was disowned. I was never to go to their town again. I was to have no contact with their friends or my siblings (who are younger than I). I would never receive help of any kind from home, with one exception: arrangements would be made with an attorney so that when I got into trouble, because "they" always do, my legal problems would be taken care of.

Among other things, I was told that I was a degenerate and would continue to sink lower and lower. Finally, my father became so abusive that I told him that if he didn't stop, I'd get out of the car. When he ordered me to stay and continued his abuse, I did get out of the car. He told me that if I didn't get back in, he'd report me to the police! I said, "There is no threat that you could make that would cause me to get back into the car and be treated like that." Seeing that he had gone too far, he backed off somewhat and I got back into the car to hear the rest of the tirade.

My mother and I had a regular exchange of unpleasant letters. Looking back, I can see that the most constructive thing that I could have done would have been to cut off all communication until I had a chance to calm down and get my problems under control. Every time I received a letter from my mother, I became so distraught that it was unbearable.

Because my "partner" was seldom available, I usually responded to these letters by seeking a partner to comfort me. The circumstances under which I found these men were not conducive to establishing a relationship and tended to exacerbate the problem. I ended up in a pattern of compulsive sexual behavior. Then, an additional problem occurred: I lost my job and had very little money saved.

Life was so unbearably painful that I often considered suicide. I was only twenty years old, had a dead-end job, no qualifications for a better job, had no one whom I could trust, knew that I was a sexual criminal and could never be accepted, couldn't control my compulsive sexual behavior, and could think of no way out. However, I hoped that somehow God would help me find a solution. Then too, I realized that if I killed myself, I would be proving to my parents that they were right. I was too angry with them to give them that satisfaction.

Somehow I was granted the strength to continue. My parents gradually began to accept me again. I broke the pattern of compulsive sexual behavior, at least temporarily. I severed my relationship with the gay men I knew, since they were not the kind of people I approved of. Because they were the only gay men I knew, I assumed that they were typical and I resolved to have no more contacts with gay men, even though I was gay. The only solution seemed to be for me to change.

I had read that the first step in changing was to become involved with "normal" people. Accordingly, I became socially involved with some Seventh Day Adventists my age. Their commitment to their faith and to a clean life were attractive. We had much in common, except that I didn't share certain aspects of their religious beliefs. However, the involvement considerably strengthened my faith and caused me to start reading the Bible.

In many respects, this was a pleasant period for me (1962-66) and was constructive, except for one problem: since my friends didn't know that I was gay, I felt like a fraud and felt somewhat isolated even when I was with them. As they gradually became married, I learned that married people have little to do with single people and that those of us who remain single are likely to experience considerable isolation.

From 1964-71, I was seeing a psychiatrist to change my affectional orientation. I became involved in an organization for single young adults in 1967, at age 29. For about four years, I dated the same woman from time to time. She was a wonderful person and could have been a good friend if I had leveled with her. However, the psychiatrist said that I would never be accepted if I were open, and therefore I shouldn't be open. The result was that I never felt accepted since I felt like a fraud.

In 1972, after I had stopped seeing the psychiatrist, another woman became emotionally involved with me. I realized then that it was wrong for me to date women in an attempt to change since the potential for hurting them was too great. Moreover, since they were looking for a husband, and it seemed clear that I would never be husband material, dating was unethical. I was forced to realize that I had no choice but to learn to accept my affectional orientation.

In 1972 I became involved with Gay House, Inc. Through it I met responsible and professional gay men, though none that I had enough in common with to establish a close relationship. Some men had accidentally become unmarried fathers in an unsuccessful attempt to change. Others had even married. Clearly, negative social attitudes toward gay men resulted in desperate attempts to change in such a way as to mess up lives. Obviously, there were millions besides me who had been victimized and suffered because of thoughtless, cruel, superstitious, and ignorant public attitudes. I developed great respect for activists who were working hard to change these attitudes, often at considerable personal risk. I felt guilty doing nothing while they were risking so much.

I was ready for action when Integrity came into existence. Louie Crew, the national founder, asked me to found a chapter in Minneapolis. Just then I was laid off from my job and had plenty of free time while the employment agencies were working. I made appointments to see priests at many Episcopal Churches in Minneapolis and got as much information from them as I could.

About the time I finished this phase of the effort, I had another job and less time to work for Integrity. We got a few interested people together for regular meetings in homes. I set up an organizing meeting at the University Episcopal Center in about November 1975, at which we got about a dozen interested participants.

Walking into that meeting took all the guts I could muster. I never had seen myself as a leader. I had minimal self-confidence, yet knew that if I could succeed in organizing an Integrity chapter, I might be able to help spare many other gay men some of the agony that I and others had suffered.

In 1978, I moved to San Diego. I've been less of an activist here, although I still become angry when I read cruel and hateful lies by "Christians" and politicians who intentionally remain ignorant. Because society has made it impossible for many of us to meet under constructive circumstances and establish permanent relationships, too many of us have been forced by loneliness into promiscuity and contracted AIDS.

Soon I will be 50. I've begun to accept that I will not likely ever have a close relationship with anyone. I lack the ability to trust others sufficiently. This hurts most when I awaken in the morning and feel so starved for affection that it is almost unbearable. Then I think of the people starving to death in Ethiopia, people suffering in wars in Central America, and people dying of AIDS without a saving knowledge of God. Knowing that I'm better off than most of the world's people and knowing that God has some plan, even though I don't understand it, gives me the necessary strength to face another day.

First Bill's Story

I am a gay priest in my early 40's and was ordained in 1974. Although I have served in the full-time parish ministry, both as a curate and as a rector, currently I work as a legal assistant and plan to go to law school. I also assist in a parish on Sundays in a non-stipendiary role. When Integrity/Chicago came into being in 1975 I was one of the charter members. I have been active in the group, to a greater or lesser extent, ever since then.

Like many Episcopalians, I was not born an Episcopalian. I came to the Episcopal Church in my middle 20's and, as with many others in our church, this resulted from an informed, adult decision. Earlier I had prepared for the priesthood in the Roman Catholic Church. I quit that pursuit and taught high school for four years, and during that time became an Episcopalian.

Several things drew me to the Episcopal Church: The solid eucharistic theology and spirituality of the Prayer Book; the beauty and majesty of the Prayer Book; the quality of the Hymnal -- theological, literary, and musical; the quality of pastoral care I received from some Episcopal priests; the social witness of Episcopalians in the areas of justice and peace; and the Anglican treatment of human sexuality, which accepted me as I was, both Christian and gay. As with many others who have found the Anglican way, I finally felt that I was "home."

Because I had found a spiritually congenial place, you may wonder why I felt it necessary to get involved with Integrity. Although Anglicanism is thoroughly catholic -- which means it is inclusive of all people and not

26

exclusive -- not everyone in the Episcopal Church understands this yet. Unredeemed human nature excludes and ranks persons as to race, clan, class, sex, wealth, sexual orientation. The way of the Gospel, as I have received it, is to be catholic -- that is, inclusive. Because some in our church follow the exclusive ways of the world, our church needs Integrity now, for two reasons.

First, straight people need Integrity to shed light on their ignorance of what homosexuality is, especially in relation to scripture and the history of the Christian church. We must correct misinformation and worse, "disinformation" about gay people.

Second, lesbians and gays need Integrity. We need to build community among ourselves; to come together for worship; and to hear the Gospel of liberation and reflect on its meaning for us, to explore how we live out that Gospel and how we bring our peculiar gifts of gayness to the high calling of advancing God's kingdom of truth, justice, and peace.

We cannot rely only on a heterosexual model; we need prayerfully and intelligently to forge a design for Christian living that works for us as gay men and lesbians. This is not a retreat into being exclusive, but simply a realistic affirmation of who we are. We are gay, we are lesbian, and we are fully members of the Body of Christ. I look for the day when nobody in our church will give a second thought to someone's being gay.

I am happy and proud to be an Anglican, and the Episcopal Church is my home. I am not leaving. I am not going anywhere else. I will stay, just as I am, in our church and pray and work for the day when all people can find in our church a safe home. Then we all together can be about our calling to advance God's kingdom and show forth God's glory.

Many have said that the Episcopal Church is "a sleeping giant" -- a small body of Christians with a potential for influence far out of proportion to our numbers. I want that giant to awaken to love and service. God could amaze us by what God can accomplish through us, in the political, economic, and social life of this nation. Grounded in Gospel compassion and justice -- and catholic inclusivity -- we could do much. Our voice would, no doubt, not be strident, but our strength would be effective in reforming systems of social and economic injustice so that the kingdom of this world would become more conformed to the kingdom of Christ. But to work together like this, as Christ would have it, we must put our own house in order first. To be credible to the world, we need to manifest justice and community that works -- among "all sorts and conditions" of persons. We need to show the world, as the civil rights movement of the 1960's put it, "Nobody is free until everybody is free."

James Mitchell's Story

The depression had hit us fairly hard and even though we lived in a rather economically well off community, Bronxville, New York, we were really dirt poor. Despite that, through the influence of friends, family and the church I managed to experience all the advantages of an upper-middle class upbringing.

The Episcopal Church was always central to my life. Many of my activities as a child and as I grew up centered around the church. I was an acolyte at Christ Church, Bronxville from as far back as I can remember. When it came to the question of college, I thought I had no chance because of finances, but through the church I received funds, funds that I did not have to pay back. My early ambitions centered on the church, and I had hoped that I might be a priest. My brother was pursuing that goal. I hoped to follow him.

When I went off to college, I had no idea that I was homosexual. Of course, I can look back now and see signs in my adolescence that clearly indicate that I was gay at an early stage, but I didn't recognize them at the time. I had girl friends in high school and when I first got to college. I enjoyed being with girls -- I still do -- but sexually girls drew from me a blank.

On discovering my sexual orientation, at first I didn't tell many people other then those gay men I found in my college town (Rochester, NY). In my junior year when I began to accept the reality in myself I also began to worry about my career choice. How could I be a priest and gay? I had heard my share of horror stories from the pulpit and from the talk of adults. No Episcopal Chaplain served the University of Rochester, and the rector of the church I attended on Sundays seemed rather distant and haughty. I had one gay friend who also aspired to the Episcopal priesthood, and he told me to forget about talking to anyone in that diocese. I don't even remember who was bishop at the time.

When I came home for vacation at Christmas, I decided I should talk to the assistant at my home church, Christ Church, Bronxville. Father Stone was very supportive and felt I should go ahead with my planned career. He just advised me not to be too open about being gay. He said the church needed to minister to gay people and that maybe that was why "I was called." I felt good after this interview. Unfortunately, no other Episcopal clergy advised me so clearly or so kindly.

The most devastating time occurred when I decided that I had to really separate myself and chose to spend a weekend at Holy Cross Monastery in West Park. I did not choose at random. I had had several positive experiences with the Holy Cross Fathers. When I was younger, I had a particularly good retreat at church during a Lenten season with a member of that order. I also had, on a number of occasions, the good fortune of meeting Father Huntington. In addition, members of my family had attended the Kent School, and all they could talk about was the wonderful Father Sill, the former headmaster and a member of the Order.

That weekend at West Park devastated me. Father Whitimore had several "talks" with me; actually he did most of the talking. He stressed that as a homosexual I certainly was not welcome in the priesthood of the Episcopal Church as far as he was concerned. He talked about sin and sex, especially about the sin of sex outside the prescribed forms. He said I was not an evil

30

person, but I must give up this sinful habit. I was too inexperienced and ignorant to respond to him as I might. I knew in my heart that I had not chosen my sexuality. It had manifested itself for as long as I could remember. Father Whitimore asked me to come and pray with him later that evening, but I was just too ashamed. After dinner I went directly to my room.

Later, I had a knock at the door and another priest of the order asked to come in. It did not take him long to get to his point: he wanted to have sex with me. How he knew I was gay I still do not know, but at the time I could only presume that Whitimore had told him. I had all I could do to get him out of my room. I promised not to tell anyone he had come on to me. I guess I've broken that promise now, but I presume that he has passed on. I was 19 or 20 at the time and he was in his 60's, more than 35 years ago. I left the next day, right after breakfast, a day early.

I never left the church, but I didn't remain active in it. I somehow knew that what I had been told was wrong, but I didn't think it was my job to do anything about changing the church. For almost 20 years I attended church on Easter and Christmas and occasionally at other times. My greatest pleasure came from the music and liturgy. I never joined a parish. In fact, I still haven't.

I did become active in the gay rights movement and while pursuing a career as a teacher did what I could to fight discrimination against gays. In the early 70's I started to attend Integrity meetings in New York City. I found for the first time many gay people who had the same interest in the Episcopal Church I used to have. There were gay priests and plenty of straight priests that supported the rights of gays. This was a place I could feel at home. I attended regularly. Some said that these meetings should not substitute for belonging to a parish. I disagreed because I saw no need for our money to go into the coffers of the church establishment. The only place I felt comfortable was at Integrity masses. I wanted my money to go there.

I looked forward to Integrity meetings every week. Often sermons related to my own existence. Previously, when I attended at a parish, I chose an early mass to avoid sermons.

In July of 1986, I was diagnosed with AIDS. A doctor had discovered a Kaposi's lesion on my foot. Even though I tested negative on the AIDS antibody tests, both the ELISA and the Western Blot, a number of physicians felt that I must have the dreaded disease. As one told me, "After all you are gay (in a high risk group) and KS is one of the CDC's opportunistic infections associated with AIDS. In fact KS is usually found only in gay men with AIDS and not in IV drug users with AIDS ."

I could not understand it at all. It seemed to me that if I had KS, then the HIV virus must have already done its thing. Why didn't I have the antibodies? No one could explain. I did not belong to one of the high risk groups for the "normal" or usual Kaposi's Sarcoma: I am not African, Mediterranean or over 60.

Medical practitioners took much blood and did all sorts of tests both simple and exotic, but to no avail. They just couldn't get the AIDS virus to grow in my blood or detect its presence. My T-4 cells were not low nor were any of the other tests at all revealing.

The worst part was mental. When you think that you only have a few years to live, everything changes. Fortunately I had the help of a good counselor, Father John McNeill, ex-S.J. His own problems with the Pope gave me strength to hope.

Some of my physical problems were mainly psychological, but I didn't know that at the time. I felt that every thing I recognized in my body signaled the disease.

In November of that year New York Integrity sponsored an AIDS memorial service at The Cathedral of St John the Divine and friends got me to go. One of them was graduating from the Parsonage program that night, and he asked me to come. I had known him for a long time and love him dearly, so I drove into the city for the service.

The service included a laying on of hands for those with AIDS, ARC or their friends. I went to the chapel with hundreds of others, and a priest anointed me.

My next appointment with a doctor was a few weeks later. This was a specialist dealing with skin cancers, particularly KS. After reviewing my case he seemed to feel that I did not have AIDS and that I fell into a small group of men who get KS, but don't fit the standard model that is described in the textbooks. Was there a connection between the sacrament of unction and the new doctor's pronouncement? I don't know.

I still go to Integrity, but am very saddened by the un-christianlike behavior of the Episcopal Church. I went to General Convention in Detroit and heard many disappointing things and realized how far we have to go before lesbians and gays are accepted as full members in this church. I regularly read letters in Episcopal publications from clergy that, in effect, are gay bashing. The "flap" over the Rev. Robert Williams has only given the gay bashers in our church and the homophobes the license to vent their bigotry and hate. The Episcopal Synod of America has scared our church leadership into all sorts of councils and meetings and this with their membership of only 20,000 to 25,000. Meanwhile, the 200,000 lesbian or gay women and men remain second-class citizens. The church creates commissions to study the subject and doesn't even appoint one member of Integrity to the commissions.

If Integrity is to provide more than just an occasional home for lesbian and gay Episcopalians, then it has to lead more forcefully. It must arrange for the ordination of practicing lesbian and gay priests. It must insist that the Church proudly bless the union of same-sex couples openly and publicly. In cities where membership is large, maybe Integrity should form parishes.

Matthew's Story

In June 1975 I experienced a profound conversion to Christianity, although I had been an active member of a congregation all my life.

In September 1975 I stood before a group of fellow parishioners and testified to the power of God. I explained that my awareness of the power of God was manifest to me in God's power to heal my homosexuality.

In November 1975 the Bishop of Colorado asked me to speak from the floor of the Diocesan Convention in opposition to a new special interest group known as Integrity. I did not speak to the Convention, but I did address a workshop on sexuality that afternoon. I came out to them as a healed homosexual and begged them not to remove my grace by condoning homosexuality or those who did.

In August 1981 I was married in the Episcopal Church to a woman I loved very much.

In August 1986 I came out to my family and my church as a practicing homosexual.

In September 1986 I left my wife.

In June 1988 I joined Integrity.

Many stories weave together to create the braid that is my life.

I cannot blame or judge. I can only hope to explain and to understand events as I have experienced them.

I must take responsibility for the fact that I, as did many others, made choices that have led to misunderstanding, hurt, and alienation.

I sought from the Church those things that the Gospels and the Church supposedly stand for: acceptance, recognition, and belonging.

I recognize now that I was willing to sell away my right to study, pray, inwardly digest, and decide--hallmarks of the Episcopal denomination.

What I was taught I accepted on faith--faith as I understood it then: a blind obedience to authority, tradition and peer pressure.

Since coming out for the second time, I have experienced direct and indirect hostility, oppression, and alienation within my family and within the church. This time, instead of hiding in fear, I have grasped firmly the opportunity to study diligently, to pray fervently, and to explore the issues carefully.

I love the Episcopal Church because of its tradition of study and because of its deep compassion for the needy. Paradoxically, until recently the Church has used our energies and talents while ignoring the realities of our existence. The Church has prescribed silence and separation for gays and lesbians.

I will not rehearse the arguments about Church teaching. That information is readily available from many fine sources. I believe that homosexuality and Christian faith are not mutually exclusive.

When I came out as a "healed homosexual," no one examined the underlying forces that motivated me to such a conclusion. No one was interested in my personal history or the wide subject of sexuality. In saying "no one," I include myself.

The Church accepted me as a symbol and exploited me as propaganda. I went along, afraid of losing the approval and acceptance that I desperately sought. When I could not sustain the illusion, I ceased to be of value for the Church's propaganda; I lost their approval. Not one of the "healers" tried to help me discover meaning within the turmoil.

The Episcopal Church encouraged me to misinform myself and others, to be silent and secretive. The secular world does the same thing to other gays.

Some have begun to change. We must continue the process of open, honest, educated dialogue, study, and prayer if the Church is to remain faithful to its high calling as the Body of Christ.

In typical fundamentalist superstition, I chose to perceive my gayness as sin. I was sitting in my apartment alone in tension between inner feeling and social pressure. "Okay," I screamed at God. "If you want me to hear you, then you will have to speak directly to me in a way that I can understand. I am going to throw this brand new bible up in the air. I will follow and believe whatever you say on the page it opens to."

The bible fell open to 1 Corinthians 6: I noticed only "....homosexuals...will not enter the kingdom of heaven..." and stopped.

How different those following years might have been had I chosen instead on the same page: "...you have been bought with a price..."

I married Donna because I loved her. We were separated not because of one issue, but because of a myriad of intricately complex problems.

We married with an understood commitment to honesty, no matter how painful, to forgiveness, no matter how hard, and to an ongoing search for the will of God in our lives.

It is the continued trust in those commitments that enables us to remain in "relationship." We meet frequently and still work very hard on those commitments. We enjoy bagels every Sunday morning before we attend church together and we share our love of music, children, people, and God with our congregation whenever possible.

Donna attends Integrity sharing her gifts, the worship, and the program with all of us.

I believe we have a great deal to say about the practice of the discipline of discipleship.

I was so nervous when I walked into my first Integrity meeting that I could barely walk or speak. I went to "give it a try." I expected to be disappointed both socially and spiritually. My skepticism lasted for the second and third meetings. It was difficult to trust the warmth and the seriousness I found there.

Integrity means a place shared with others like me who are supportive, concerned, and challenging. It means a place to worship in an environment of inclusivity. It is a home base which empowers me to face the world as a gay person and as a spiritual person.

More important, Integrity is a forum. Unlike the Church in general, Integrity provides a space where issues are confronted in clarity.

In other settings, issues divide as "we-they," with little if any recognition that the "they" are actually present. Issues are easily intellectualized into banality or obscurity.

Most of us in Integrity are acutely aware of a greater "we" that we have been excluded from, yet regularly participate in. We hope to see the Church grow into ever greater wholeness.

I am proud to be a member of Integrity, proud of the deep spiritual commitment to understanding the will of God, proud of the genuine and difficult commitment to acceptance and understanding, proud of a Church that is brave enough and willing enough to remain in dialogue with those who have for so long been displaced, rejected, and hopeless.

I am gay. I am Christian. And my story continues to unfold.

Kathleen's Story

I have always known the love of Christ in my life. From the moment my loving parents brought me to the font of baptism, the Holy Spirit has been with me as my Comforter and Guide. What faith my parents had and expectations too, that their first born, a daughter, who was an answer to their prayers, would be all that they hoped and desired.

With the ordinary ups and downs of life, I did become all that my parents had hoped for ... a mother of four beautiful children, a caring wife, active in my church, attentive to my elderly grandparents and unfailing in my devotion to my parents. I knew that my parents un conditionally loved me.

But something happened. At age 35, my friendship with a woman I met in church brought a revelation which forever changed my life and the lives of those around me.

When I accepted myself and acknowledged my homo- sexuality, I experienced a joy and peace which I had never known. In my new wholeness, I faced an incredi- ble dilemma: what would happen to the relationships around me?

My whole world turned upside down. My orientation set off a bomb in my family, my church, and my com- munity. My whole support structure tumbled. After 20 years in an "enlightened" college community, I had one friend left, and she was afraid to support me because of her husband.

All that I was, all that I had done, suddenly meant nothing. My church quickly excommunicated me, and my family, without so much as a word, cut me off. My children hid from me in public. In the span of a mere sentence, I had lost much of what was important to me. Was this lesbian part of me worth losing so much?

In times of trouble, my support had always come from my church and from my family. Now that I was in the biggest need of my life, neither was there. I sought help from a clergy counselor, who suggested clearing out my savings and moving to Tahiti....and he wasn't kidding! I'm not that kind of person. I continued to look for an answer.

Matters worsened. I even had to go to court to see my two minor children. Hysteria surged. Fear, ignorance, and prejudice ran rampant. Feeling totally devoid of any self-worth, I agreed to joint custody of my two minor kids, with the primary care given by their father. He had the house and a car and a job. I had no support, no education, and barely enough self-esteem to continue. By now you should ask, "Is this woman deranged, or what???"

That was January 1986. After I signed the custody papers, my partner and I moved to Denver. By the grace of God, we started attending St. Barnabas Episcopal Church, where we found the healing love of Christ. That congregation took us in and ministered to our physical and emotional needs like angels from heaven. Young and old alike accepted us, encouraged us, prayed for us, and brought a miracle into our lives. Our faith was reaffirmed, and it was with great joy that we were confirmed into the Episcopal Church. We were surely no longer outcasts, and we had a "family" again.

The pain and conflict we had experienced had truly been the grace of God in our lives, and we know now what it means to walk daily by faith.

We have our own home now, the prospects of a bright professional future for my partner and strangely, it would seem, sole custody of the two minor children. God has honored my commitment by allowing me to serve in Integrity. I praise God and look forward to the time when my parents can acknowledge that the baby whom they welcomed at baptism is still their loving daughter.

God's love comes to me through all fellow members of our Episcopal Church, brothers and sisters in Christ.

Jack's Story

At twelve, I began to have those sexual feelings that all teenagers have, but I wasn't attracted to girls. This disturbed and confused me.

My family were strict fundamentalist Pentecostals, so I completely put homosexual desire out of my mind, but it always lurked just below the surface.

Being homosexual was not something that I learned -- it was just who I was. As a teenager I had no homosexual contacts (even though I wanted to) because I was too afraid. I felt that God would take this desire away. I spent years and years praying and pretending to be heterosexual. Eventually I married, hoping marriage would finally cure me of these supposedly unnatural desires.

Only at the age of thirty, with many miserable years of denying my true self, did I discover I had lived a lie since I was twelve years old. I was very unhappy. Finally I admitted to myself and then slowly to others that I was gay. It was a hard decision to make as I knew it would mean losing life as I knew it. I might lose my children and many friends who would not accept my true identity. But I could not go on pretending to be someone that I wasn't.

I knew I would never truly be happy and fulfilled until I became the real me. Heterosexuals don't force themselves to love persons of the opposite sex, they just do: if you are gay, you are gay.

Why would anyone choose to practice a way of life so looked down on by many in our church and in society?

Contrary to popular belief, no one chooses sexual orientation.

It isn't important whom you love, but that you love.

Gay and lesbian Episcopalians are everywhere in the church. We serve as bishops, priests, lay readers, acolytes and monetary supporters. It is time for the church to recognize us as the important providers that we are and recognize our right to be who we are. What kind of people would force us to hide even though they know we are there?

I am thankful for the Episcopal Church as it has made great strides in seeking justice for all God's children, not only for lesbians and gays. I support my Cathedral of Grace and Holy Trinity in Kansas City. Our Cathedral feeds over 150 hot meals each day to people in Kansas City who would otherwise not eat. It is that kind of love that I sense in the Episcopal Church that makes me proud to be a member of this church and of Integrity.

Jeff's Story

The church -- or at least the priests -- said little or nothing about sexuality when I was growing up in an Episcopal parish during the 1960's and early 70's, in a suburb of Chicago. Marriage was, of course, proper, but I don't remember hearing any sermons that dealt with sexuality.

No one exposed me to the categories of moral vs. immoral, straight vs. gay, as these things simply weren't discussed. As a result, when I discovered I was gay, I never felt guilty about it. Likewise, my family considered it improper to talk about sex. Since morality seemed to get confused with sex, my family did not discuss morality either. About the only thing I was taught at home was that marriage was better than being single. It was like growing up in a vacuum.

Because of all these non-influences, I had no choice but to begin making up my own mind on ethical and moral issues. I read Washington, Jefferson and Lincoln, and added the Ten Commandments and the Golden Rule.

During college I started to realize that I might be gay. I read as many books as I could to "research" the topic thoroughly. When it was clear to me that I was indeed gay, I looked to the books for guidance. I did not look to the church, or my family, or the clergy -- my experience simply had taught me not to expect guidance from any of those sources.

Currently, I am a member of a small north-side church in Chicago, which I attend infrequently. I do, however, attend Integrity services regularly. It has nothing to do with churchmanship -- I could go to a "high" church or to a "low" church; it would not matter. It has to do, not with the type of service, but with the type of people.

Integrity/Chicago manifests a definite feeling of community. While gay people attend many parishes too, there they seem to be closeted. I want to worship with openly gay/lesbian people -- and also, I want to do volunteer work with and for gay/lesbian people and the gay/lesbian community. I don't want to be discreet (which being translated means "guarded"), as I would have to be at a regular parish. I want to be candid, affirming.

Some say: "Be nice and quiet and tasteful, and the good, liberal, straight people will give us our rights." I believe that we must stand up for our rights.

I want to make a direct contribution to the gay/lesbian community. Integrity lets me do so.

Joe's Story

I often feel out of place as a Christian in the midst of the gay subculture. The gay press, specifically *The Advocate* (the most influential gay news publication in the United States) has a decidedly New Age, and anti-Christian, point of view. Reading this and local gay news, one could believe that *Christian* from a gay perspective, means "closed-minded and intolerant."

Our Episcopal publications have made me feel just as alien. I read letters from people who quote easy one-liners from Scripture and say "See? God condemns homosexuals."

To be a gay person in a Christian subculture, or a Christian in a gay subculture, is difficult. I am not the only gay person I know who has found it necessary to seek counseling for just this reason. In fact, society -- especially Christian society -- has had the same effect on many gay Christians I know.

When I first learned a term for the feelings, I was involved in an exciting high school group and a youth singing group, both at church. The singing group was popular with the parishioners, and none of us felt any lack of love. The high school group evolved into a college group, and promoted a good sense of family.

Sexual yearnings are strong at that age, but I was sure that doing anything about mine would be wrong. Ignoring those urges seemed the easiest thing to do. Since I had no sexual interest in women, I sought out other gay Episcopalians and discussed my feelings with them.

I also talked with people I loved and respected. This was usually a good experience, as most of my friends, counselors, and priests were supportive and understanding. I realized that it was time to venture into the gay world at last, but I didn't know how to break into the social life of the subculture and meet people who shared my love for God.

I started counseling and going to Dignity, a gay and lesbian Roman Catholic organization. Dignity in Tucson was not what I hoped it would be in terms of community, but I met my love there, as many people seem to do. He and I worked together on the music for the Eucharists. We learned that we had much in common in our dedication to the Church. Being Roman Catholic and Episcopalian made our ideas fairly compatible.

In counseling I learned to recognize what can and what cannot be changed. For instance, I can decide whom to listen to and believe regarding my sexual life. I cannot, on the other hand, change all society's views at one time. I also learned that coming out to friends, family, and co-workers can be liberating. By doing so, I stopped self-oppression and passed the supposed burden to those to whom it belongs.

My road to salvation has been somewhat easier than that of many other gay Christians. I safely put aside my sexual feelings during the difficult years of adolescence. I realized in time that when a girlfriend's mother started talking about marriage I had to make a quick exit. I have rarely faced rejection. I was fortunate to connect with my beloved three years ago, with a minimum of bar-hopping.

Many people have problems reconciling a Christian faith with their God-given ability to love. That's why I am active in Integrity. I am proud to be involved in the Episcopal expression of Christianity because people listen and care about the problems of gay people.

At the last diocesan convention, a priest who has known me since I was eight years old, ignored me. In past years he and his wife nearly ran to greet me, but this year they had received Integrity information with my name on it. Suddenly I became invisible.

I have been gay all along -- I knew I was different even at the age of eight -- but now I wasn't being a good boy and hiding.

I wish we did not need Integrity, but for now we do.

Mary's Story

"You shouldn't spend so much time with Sarah; it's *unnatural*!"

My mother's words echo in my ears 35 years later. I was 17 and only dimly aware of what my feelings meant. All I knew was that I was crazy about Sarah and wanted to be with her all the time. I was jealous when she went out on dates with boys. I didn't enjoy dating.

Then in college it happened again. I fell in love with Anne. How my heart would beat when we were together! I still didn't have a name for my feelings, but I knew they were unnatural and terrifying.

Majoring in religion, I hoped to work with young people in a church setting. My studies of the Bible confirmed my mother's pronouncements and my own worst fears: women loving women was a SIN. How could I, a born-again Christian and a granddaughter of two Methodist ministers, have such feelings?

So I dated a few boys and eventually married, knowing that my feelings for my husband were not the same as what I'd felt for Sarah and Anne. But to acknowledge those carefully hidden feelings for women would have been anathema. I *knew* that homosexuality was weird and sinful. I had learned society's lessons well, and so I made peace with my life as wife and mother despite intense attractions to women that continued.

Two decades later, my husband left me, hoping to find the woman of his dreams. I would never have sought a divorce, but after we had separated, I began to realize how relieved I was--and how lucky! With the love and support of friends and family, I embarked on a new career and began the next chapter of my life. Now free to explore my feelings for women, I became aware of the beauty, power, and persistence of those feelings throughout my life. Once again I found myself deeply attracted to my women friends and I wondered if perhaps I might really be a lesbian. Just thinking that word, the "L_____ word," prompted panic. But with the help of my therapist, I began to unravel what it might mean. Still uncertain, I attended "singles" groups, but always found myself seeking out the *women* there. As I started acknowledging my lesbian feelings, my life began to open up to a new dimension.

Then Marie appeared, and it was clear to both of us that God had brought us together. But would God bless our love for one another? I was frantic! All the old negative tapes played loud and clear while I desperately sought guidance and support for my journey as a Christian and a lesbian. I read every book I could find, every pamphlet, every relevant Bible verse. I wrote away for information; I talked to my pastor. And I prayed -- oh, how I prayed--because I was scared to death that God would not approve of my relationship with Marie, even though it had the blessing of both my children and my friends.

Enter Integrity. A small ad in the paper announced the initial meeting of this group for gay and lesbian Episcopalians and their friends. At last, a place where I could meet other gay and lesbian Christians! I timidly ventured to that first gathering and knew I had found a home. Here was a group of Christians who dared to proclaim that God made and loves each of us the way we are and, like a lover, calls us to embrace God and one another. That is Good News indeed!

First David's Story

This is the standard speech I give when I tell people why I'm an Episcopalian.

I was not brought up in any organized (or even unorganized) religion. When I first set foot in an Episcopal church I was twenty-one, an almost complete stranger to the Church, and had been out of the closet as a gay man for six years.

Because I came into the church as an adult, I probably have not had some of the same difficult struggles with hurtful parishes or dioceses, or with my identity as a Church member, as have some of my cradle Episcopalian friends. I have been able to choose what I wanted in a parish, and I have been able to choose what I wanted in a church. I have been lucky enough to live in a diocese that allowed me that freedom.

I first attended an Episcopal service about eight years ago at the invitation of my landlords at the time, two gay Episcopal priests. The parish was a small inner-city parish in a large Midwestern town. The church was a large red brick building of traditional design. It had been built to be the cathedral for its diocese. The worship was Anglo-Catholic, and indeed the intense "churchiness" of the entire experience was one of the things that initially drew me to that church. I am not a very mystically-inclined person, but the dark wooden pews, the shadowy vaulted ceiling, and the altogether novel smell of incense helped me to get in touch with a part of myself that admitted the existence in my life of a certain amount of mystery.

While the parish was what most Episcopalians I know would call very high-church, it did not neglect spirituality at the expense of liturgy and trappings. The froufrou, the "smells and bells," were an addition to the worship but not the focus of it. The congregation was about half black, and also half gay. People came from the neighborhood, an inner-city poor black neighborhood, and from the suburbs. The congregation included very wealthy and very poor people, professionals and residents of halfway houses for the mentally ill.

This church provided a feeling of community on many levels, racial, social and sexual, that I have not found in any parish since then. By this I mean not only that the different races, economic levels and sexual orientations were represented there, but also that this church *was* these differences. I have seen parishes since then that, while admitting worshipers of many different kinds, have remained intensely themselves. I think that it is not enough for the Church to be open to these sorts of differences. The Church must become these differences. It is not a question of why there aren't more blacks, gays, etc., in the Church, but of why the Church doesn't reconcile with and encompass these differences.

This is, I think, one of the great strengths of the Episcopal Church, its ability to reconcile. Such steps as the recognition of Integrity as an official participant in the national Church and the ordination of women as priests (and now as bishops, thanks to Barbara Harris and the Holy Spirit,) are not only politically correct steps to take but are crucial to the continued vitality and perpetuation of the Gospel message and critical to helping people to think well of themselves.

A second consideration I have had in being a member of the Episcopal Church is that it is a church which makes me feel good. The parishes which I have belonged to have been ones that have made a special effort to welcome those people who have often been disenfranchised.

At the first parish I attended, there was a woman who, during the exchange of the Peace, made a special effort to exchange the Peace with those people in the congregation that she couldn't stand. This is what the Church needs to do. One of the great attractions of the Episcopal Church for me is its emphasis on redemption rather than on regulation. This is crucial for people who, for any reason, do not get the validation which everyone needs.

I believe that the need to be part of a "we" is one of the most important needs that humans have. To deny someone access to a "we," for any reason, doesn't help the person to feel better about self.

This is an issue that the lesbian and gay community wrestles with too. At the last Lesbian/Gay Pride Day parade in San Francisco a visible group of transvestites drew much attention. Many people thought that the lesbian and gay community should tone down such "extreme" elements since, being the most visible, they draw some of the most audible criticism. But I believe that lesbians and gays should be the last group to say that such harmless behavior is inappropriate. I think that the right to public expression of one's identity needs to be nearly unlimited, and I think the Church needs to respect and nurture that right.

What's the point of all this? I'm not saying that all parishes should become liturgically oriented, or that parishes should aim for a quota of minority members. What I think we need to do as parishes and as individuals is to work towards overcoming our "instinctive" fears about people and behaviors that are different from our own. Parishes need to make it known as best they can that they welcome anyone--women, gays, physically and mentally challenged, members of racial minorities, criminals--*anyone* to participate fully in the life of the Church. They need to advertise in local papers, in diocesan papers, in neighborhood papers, in papers in these special communities, that all people are welcome. The Church needs to change.

By welcoming differences into my life, I have grown. By welcoming differences into our parishes, our parishes will grow. By welcoming differences into itself, the Church can change, can remain alive. Only by welcoming everyone can the Episcopal Church keep its prayer Common, not exclusive. For the Church to remain the "good old" Episcopal Church would be for it to stagnate, to disserve a majority of its potential adherents, and to fail to promote the gospel message to its fullest.

Dennis's Story

I knew deep inside me that I was not experiencing the same thrill and excitement that my male schoolmates, my cousins, and friends were, when we got together to talk about "girls." I thought that I was shy and would eventually overcome it, so I went along with the teenage rituals of dating, going to dances, parties, movies, even sitting in the back row of the balcony, putting my arm around my date's shoulders, kissing goodnight, etc. But I finally had to admit to myself that I was not feeling anything. These young women were good friends, but I felt nothing more than a warm friendship towards them.

I developed a totally different affection for members of my own sex. This affection on the surface appeared to be admiration and idolizing. I also wanted them sexually.

The past three generations of my family have been raised as "High Anglicans" -- bells and smells Anglicans -- and I was aware of what my family considered an abomination, what was unclean, what was unnatural. When I did stop denying it and admitted to myself that I am a homosexual, I had to deal with guilt and shame.

"Why me, Lord? Why did you make me a homosexual? Why did you give me this cross to bear?"

I decided that I would get as much information as I could on my condition. Was it a phase I was going through? Would I grow out of it? I read any material I could get my hands on about sexuality and human behavior.

Whenever I found a book on this subject, the first thing I would do was to turn to the index at the back and look under "H" to see if there was anything written inside on homosexuality. I read much in those days because I wanted to learn as much as I could, but even more vitally, because I had no one to confide in.

I endured the occasional "fag" joke in silence. My siblings grew up and got married. People asked, "So when are you going to get hitched?" I am the eldest in my family. "Guess it's your turn next, Dennis," they said. These remarks embarrassed me. Mom and Dad assumed I was just not the marrying kind, and they would defend me: "Oh, he's just being picky--he's looking for the right person." Little did they know how correct they were.

I questioned whether the God who had made me would abandon me to a life of ridicule and shame. I guess in my sub-conscious I know that it wasn't God who had abandoned me; it was society and the law-makers of the Church who had.

I decided that if the Christian faith would not accept me, then I would search out other religions. I felt that if I could not worship my God as an Anglican, as a Christian, then I would do so as a member of any other religion where I should feel accepted. It seemed the thing to do at the time. All the celebrities were doing it: Sammy Davis, Jr. had converted to Judaism, Cassius Clay became a Muslim and changed his name to Mohammad Ali. I wanted to find a religion, a niche, where I could hide, not a religion which wanted to change me into something alien.

Ironically, this process reinforced my faith in God. Whatever my sexual orientation, I cannot run away from it. It is integral. Although I wallowed in self-pity, looking for someone to blame, I came to realize that the God of all the religions of this world, known by whatever name, is a loving, caring God. God does not hate me. God does not reject me. Misdirected followers cause all the hate and anger by their self-proclaimed and self-righteous interpretation of God's word.

I admitted to myself that if God made me this way, then I cannot be "sick" or "intrinsically disordered" as the Vatican recently declared. My homosexuality is not a "cross to bear" after all, but a gift, a gift to share.

I decided to stay within the Anglican Church and, with the help of my colleagues in Integrity, to try to bring about a change through a program of education and through being a visible role-model. In addition to being a member of an Anglican parish, my participation in Integrity is my idea of stewardship. The Scriptures tell us: "Our gifts differ according to the grace given us. If your gift is prophecy, then use it as your faith suggests; if administration, then use it for administration; if teaching, then use it for teaching."

The Chinese say that the longest journey begins with the first step. The members of Integrity are aware that our goal may not be accomplished in our lifetime, but it is a journey that we have freely devoted ourselves to. We truly believe that what we are doing is, in a small way, the first step on our journey to educate the Church and society.

Lesbians and gay men are first of all human beings. We contribute to society as lawyers, doctors, politicians, priests, nuns, your brother, your sister, or perhaps the person sitting in the next pew.

Contrary to the stereotype, most lesbians and gays strive for loving, monogamous relationships. We go through the dating ritual, we select a partner, we "set up house," we quarrel, we fight, we laugh, we cry, we make love, we make up, sometimes we break up. These events could happen in any relationship whether homosexual or heterosexual. The only difference between "us" and heterosexuals is our sexual partner. Why is the sex act, which is the fulfillment of a loving union between two persons who are committed to each other, considered by some to be morally evil when the two persons concerned are of the same gender?

When I told my family that I was planning to speak to my congregation about my homosexuality, they asked, "Do you really want to put yourself in that situation?" They were concerned with the possibility of a negative response. I asked why they assumed a negative response. They answered, "Not everyone would be comfortable with your discussing anything as personal as your sexuality. Some still think that sexual activity should only be between man and woman for the purpose of procreation. They may not consider homosexuality as 'natural'."

Natural? What is natural, and by whose standards? What is more natural: the two men who live around the corner in a loving commitment to each other, or the husband and wife who live next door who shout obscenities at each other and physically abuse each other in front of their children? Some may feel this is not a fair comparison. But what is the issue here anyway? Isn't it human relationships? Does not God intend for all to be compassionate, loving, and caring? Is not that God's Hope, God's Shalom?

All human relationships should have depth, commitment, caring, justice. From my personal experience, I know that these qualities can and do exist in most homosexual relationships. Some couples in our group have been together for over ten years. One couple recently celebrated 25 years of love and support for each other.

Recently a reporter for TV interviewed a group of church members threatening to leave their church if it supported lesbians and gays. The reporter asked the group whether any of them had met or spoken to a lesbian or gay person. One fellow answered, "Are you kidding? If we were seen talking to them, others would think that we were just like them."

Integrity, Dignity, and other support groups are vital means to understanding homosexual persons and to eliminating homophobia.

Call not unclean anyone whom God has made.

Barry's Story

At 30 I came to Arizona to take a job at a University. I had lived in a rural part of Australia, in small communities where I was often reminded that it would be preferable for all concerned if I kept my homosexuality to myself. I kept it to myself. I was raised an Anglican and remained involved with the church, although in a rather distant way. I cannot remember ever hearing homosexuality mentioned, positively or negatively, from the pulpit of an Anglican church in Australia.

Coming to Arizona seemed to promise the ultimate liberation. I could meet people in bars, I could join groups, possibly I could even develop a relationship. I might form friendships with people not so destructively affected by being gay as the few fellow travelers I'd en countered in Australia. So I began to find out all about it. At much the same time, I was strongly drawn to a parish which provided at least some continuity with my Australian past. I was "out" on Saturday night, but firmly back in the closet on Sunday morning, an existence not different from the one I had known in Australia, yet it troubled me: could I reconcile Saturday night with Sunday morning? As my working compromise, I convinced myself that I could exploit the bars in a sincere search for a companion, but the compromise was an uneasy one because it was to hard to apply. The compromise also frightened, because death already stalked the night in the form of AIDS. I felt very much a stranger in the cynical, vacuous ambience of the bars.

Saturday night and Sunday morning refused to remain discrete. I kept meeting the church organist and later some fellow members of the congregation in the gay meeting places. In his sermons, the rector stressed that the parish would not ostracize homosexuals. This gradually led to the gathering of a group of valued gay friends at church and to the re-founding of Integrity in our city with the support of the parish clergy. The one crucial thing it seemed that the parish could not provide was the chance for me to find a relationship. Therefore the bars still served a purpose for me, my concern over their corrupting influence matched by a my fear of isolating myself from my only chance of finding a lasting companion.

Going to the bars with looks and age less than fashionable can leave a person feeling considerably less than special. I have generally felt fortunate to have as much defense as I have against those feelings. Spending my twenties outside gay society, relying on myself to generate a non-sexual but worthwhile social life: these things gave me a resilient identity and the ability to survey the environment from a distance. After I had visited some of the bars for long enough, I realized that many fellow bar-goers made much more frequent use of the bars than I did; some of them spent three nights or more a week there, standing alone and almost never talking to others. How could such people retain any self-esteem?

Hesitantly, I began to look into this, forcing myself to be more outgoing, to get people talking in the face of resistance. The people I met in that way ranged broadly in physical attractiveness, in income and in intellect. Not all were convinced that they were strictly gay in orientation. But all were lonely, and all had some form of self-destructive behavior. One of the first people I met in this way turned on me one day and asked why I had ever bothered speaking to him. One has experienced psychiatric problems, and another may already have committed suicide. The culminating point made by this set of episodes came one Christmas Eve when I called at the bar to see whether a friend was to be alone for Christmas. Gone was the usual ambience of the place, and in its stead hung a particularly disturbing and contagious sort of gloom. As I left, a young man approached. I did not know him. He began to plead with me to let him come home with me. I offered to take him home, but somehow my intention of going to church first got in the way.

The Church of my experience in Arizona represents the practice of Christian principle and love. As I have attempted to convey, the antithesis of such principle and love seems to operate, if only for lack of imagination, in some manifestations of gay society I have experienced. The resultant alienation permits and even fosters the loneliness, the promiscuity and even the spread of AIDS. If I accept these things as inevitable, if I foster them myself, then I cannot reconcile Saturday night and Sunday morning. Whatever else my spirituality may entail, Christian spirituality must constrain my interactions with other people.

I did not choose my sexuality, and I believe that my being gay cannot be construed as a basis for the denial of spiritual possibilities by church or individual. Rather, God gives me my own set of social opportunities, and I may choose to use or misuse those opportunities. God also gives me spiritual guidance in making the choice.

Wayne's Story

The male statue appealed to me, yet I knew the other third-graders looking at the book thought the female statue would appeal to me. Nobody spoke much about "queers" in my family, community, or at church. The silence and occasional jokes made it seem horrible.

So, since I couldn't be the way I actually was, sexually and physically, I tried to be "spiritual," which for me at the time meant "non-physical." I tried to live in my mind and in prayer. I spent as much time as I could in books and at church. No one told me the good news that God made all and declared all creation to be "very good." No one expressed in a believable way the Gospel that God too had become flesh and blood.

I could repress the life God gave me only for so long. Despite the fact that society had taught me to hate my sexuality and my body, I needed love and love's joys. I couldn't be asexual, and I wouldn't accept my gayness; so, I tried to be heterosexual.

I tried dating women...being a proper gentleman and Christian, of course. But it was an effort and an act, and didn't help. Finally in desperation while in college, I bought the idea that sex with a woman would set all aright. But the only way I could keep from embarrassing myself was to think of the guy I was in love with while making love to the woman I was dating. Still I figured that if only I could find a girl I loved.....

I dated other women and hurt some dear friends.

Maybe it fails because sex outside marriage is "wrong," I thought, so I need to marry...

Thank God, I never went that far and thus avoided ruining the life of one of my girlfriends, just to try to save myself from being a pariah.

My deep involvement with and commitment to God continued. Worship and private prayer gave comfort to a lonely life; trying to understand scripture filled time and gave meaning. I used religion to avoid a major area of my life.

Others affirmed my lay ministry and wondered why I didn't seek ordination. In college I heard God's call in my own prayers and talked to my bishop. In great anguish, I even talked about my "bisexuality." He accepted me as a postulant on the condition that I get into therapy.

Seminary and therapy were helpful and good. I grew a bit and learned much. Yet I understood my solemn vows of ordination in an anti-gay sense. That "faith" coupled with my therapist's views reinforced my suppression so thoroughly that sometimes I could go for three or four years without a "lapse."

After ordination as deacon and then priest, I continued in therapy because I knew I had not changed. I had only suppressed. I continued to abuse myself in this way for seven more years.

Then Integrity wrote me. I was terrified: How could such a far-away organization know I was gay? The mailing had in fact gone to all the clergy of the Diocese, but I couldn't even ask anyone else about such things then. When I finally had the courage to read the literature (behind locked doors at home two weeks later), it set me on a pilgrimage that took three years as I read and prayed alone and afraid.

One day in my prayers, it occurred to me that I had done everything I could to change: years of anguished prayer, anointing, confession, thousands of dollars and painful self-examination in therapy with three excellent therapists and two therapy groups. When faced with failure, a fanatic keeps trying the same thing, only harder. It was time to try something else.

I never chose to be gay; it was a gift, a rare rose with some thorns. My reading and my experience convinced me that I was not crazy enough to have chosen the rejection and danger that our society heaps on its lesbian and gay citizens.

I discovered that while some passages in scripture oppose homosexual practice connected with Baalism or prostitution, our culture ignores the sexual undertones which fill the story of David and Jonathan. Likewise, we have lost sight of the fact that Jesus and the Old Testament prophets considered the sin of Sodom and Gomorrah to be the gross mistreatment of defenseless guests. We never allow what Jesus calmly accepted when John rested his head on Jesus' chest during the Last Supper.

It was time to leave the small-town congregation I had loved, enjoyed, and served for ten years. I knew that with my new understanding of what God wanted in my life, I should leave the South and this Diocese that was afraid of single clergy--there were two of us. But the Bishop and a congregation in a large city asked me to reconsider them after I had declined their call. We had enjoyed each other, and our gifts, needs, and commitments matched amazingly well. So, in spite of personal risk, I accepted their call.

Looking for a relationship is hard for most people, but it is especially hard when you're a public figure, secretly gay. Going to bars seemed inappropriate and foolish. After months of meeting no one, I trusted my secret to a non-gay priest friend who had lesbians and gays in his congregation. He introduced me to a gay couple who began inviting me to their home and introducing me to their friends.

I'll never forget my first date. Suddenly all the things I had gone through for years--making plans, bringing flowers, kissing good-night at the door--came alive and were right. Sometimes I regret the years I had wasted; but mostly I rejoice at the joy of coming home for the first time. I had always been angry at myself for never being able to say to the women I dated and cared for, "I love you." Now I did, to a man.

I met the man with whom I wanted to share my life. He was religious and involved with the Metropolitan Community Church. He had gifts and a personality different from mine. We had enough in common to understand one another, but plenty of differences to keep things spicy and growing. After several months we moved in together and began sharing the daily joys of life: cooking for each other, building a patio together, helping the neighbors put up a fence, and having friends and parishioners over to supper.

We went slowly with my congregation. A gay bishop gave us a key: he said that people have been taught that "homos" are dangerous, immoral, and ugly people. Let folks get to know you, and they'll dismiss the idea

67

that you could be a faggot. When Andy finally moved in with me, there was some talk but no trouble in the parish, for people knew and cared for both of us. We had a great five years with that congregation. Andy was a deacon in the Metropolitan Community Church but would sing for us when that wasn't a conflict. We had a weekly prayer breakfast and a prison ministry that we both participated in.

Five years later, I was leading a retreat for the Diocese and my partner was spending the weekend with his birth family at their lake house, when someone broke into our home and along with a radio, some rings, and cash, took the strongbox in which we kept our letters to one another. The broken box was found--the letters read and taken to the bishop with threats. If I would resign quickly and quietly, the Bishop would help me find a congregation in another diocese. We shook on it. He made three phone calls, and I went home to tell my partner and write my vestry and people.

I thank God for three things: 1) A network of laity, deacons, priests, and bishops (some old friends, but many strangers) who cared for and helped us during my year of jobless wandering. 2) Air fares were low enough for me to meet with call committees and bishops in several dioceses scattered all over the nation. 3) People supported me with prayer, especially Andrew and my former congregations.

It seems that about a third of my congregation had known that I was gay and did not care. Another third seems to have wondered but had dismissed the idea since we were not evil or strange. A final third could not think of a bachelor priest as sexual. These last were the ones most upset and hurt by the truth and by my resignation. When the bishop appointed a new pastor, I left town to allow them to get on with their lives.

I found a home in a convent in a large city whose bishop had offered regular supply work. He also put my name before call committees. I was able to live in the guest house and helped occasionally in the office of a nearby congregation. The courage and kindness of that bishop, that rector and his gay lover, and that community still inspire me. While there, the widows and ladies in my former congregation who had been in the custom of having me to supper each month, now asked my partner to join them. Andy remained to take care of our house and support us financially.

After nearly a year, I had a couple of offers and so was able to accept a congregation that is a good match rather than having to take just any work. We've worked together now for four years for the Reign of Christ. But I have not yet shared my gayness with them, so strong is the fear, mistrust, and hurt that culminated in my life when I was forced to resign.

Clergy who come out to their people tend to have to spend the rest of their ministry in that congregation. New congregations are often afraid even to consider an openly gay priest.

I rejoice to be in a diocese where people treat me naturally. They care more about the quality of my spirit than about whether I am gay. I wonder how I survived all those years in a homophobic diocese and region. I pray for those lesbian and gay laity and clergy who serve Christ and our denomination so faithfully in those areas where hate is nourished.

Carla's Story

Since I was my parents' only child, and the only girl in three generations on either side of my family, they raised me to be perfect. I think I complied with all the rural, plain, and simple taboos of my conservative family. I was born over 40 years ago in a tiny midwestern town of 300 rigid and religious souls.

We attended church seven hours a week: Fundamentalist, sure. I didn't know anything else. What the preacher said that he got out of the King James Bible became what we talked about in Sunday School and at Sunday dinner and Wednesday supper and when we did family prayers every night. The preacher spoke much about drinking and dancing and cards and hell fires that would never go out. God was a man with a white beard, sitting on a cloud, breathing smoke out of his nostrils. He carried lightning bolts and threw them at people who did wrong. A girl in my elementary school got hit by lightning, and we all knew it happened because she had sinned.

When I graduated from high school, I got a scholarship. I was the first person on either side of my family to go away to the university. People warned me about the sin in my college town, and they were mostly right. My denomination did not have a congregation within walking distance of my dormitory, so I went to the Christian Church. They had a big choir and I joined. One of the people in the choir was a girl named Carla -- my name, too. She was shy and came from a town similar to my own. We were best friends -- my first friend who wasn't a relative. The next year we roomed together in the all-girls' dorm. It was like heaven, having a "sister," a woman, a person I could talk to for the first time in my life. I could trust her. She trusted me. We were alone in an evil world of sex and drink and drugs. We didn't need that stuff: we had each other.

Some of the women on our floor started a rumor that Carla and I were lesbians and sex partners. The first time I heard that, I threw up. Lesbians were fat, hairy women who had bad complexions and talked dirty. They wore T-shirts without any bras and had whistles on a lanyard around their necks. They were all in physical education. They all had social diseases. They were rotten and doomed to perdition and the fiery lakes of hell. I was not a lesbian and Carla was not a lesbian. We were both size eights; we were both quiet and polite and proper. We wore clean clothes. I got sick. Carla laughed.

Carla and I roomed together for five years. We both got Masters' degrees and teacher certifications. When we found jobs we were only 35 miles apart. Every weekend, one of us would visit the other. For eight months, we looked forward to that last hour on Friday. Then Carla's grandmother died, and I knew how close they had been. I drove over at once to see Carla and we held each other for over two hours. We both cried.

I went to the funeral in the funeral home and afterwards Carla took me with her to her grandmother's house where the relatives and neighbors had brought in dinner. She gave me a cup and saucer of her grandmother's as a keepsake. The whole family was friendly and welcoming. They asked me to stay over that night. I shared a bed with Carla.

In the middle of the night, Carla started to shake and to sob again. I held her. And we became lovers.

71

That was over fifteen years ago. We are still lovers.

On all the earth I can love no one else as much as I love Carla. No one else, anywhere, loves me as much as Carla does. We have one strong and beautiful soul, and we care for other people because we care so much for each other. We are both great teachers, and we love our kids and our colleagues with a huge love. People invite us both to dinners and to parties together now, even in our rural midwestern town (we're now teaching at the same school). We don't try to hide anything from anybody anymore. We don't make a big scene about our love, either. We don't have to.

I can look in the mirror and see a lesbian now. And I can call Carla a lesbian without getting sick. And I discovered that God loves us more for being honest than for trying to conceal the simple truth and be something we aren't. It is worse trying not to be somebody you are than trying to be somebody you aren't. We don't have to bother any more.

Six years ago on February 14, we celebrated our union with a major occasion. We had talked about such a celebration for years and finally met an Episcopal chaplain at our alma mater who is a gay male priest. We talked with him for a year about marriage and holy unions and recommitment and fidelity and love and all the implications.

We came to realize that priests and ministers do not "marry" people -- only the partners do. The couple makes vows to one another in the presence of God and their friends, and everyone prays that they will be faithful and happy. We saw that it is the love and fidelity, the covenant, which brings us together and keeps us together, and that sex is a major and beautiful part of that union.

We discovered a God who loves and creates and nurtures like a mother and a loving father, and not a God who hates and judges and kills. And we found a God who gives us minds to think with about good and evil, and trust and pretense -- and not just a closed book. We found a God who loves us, and loves through us. We were confirmed in the Episcopal Church in 1982 and are both very active.

Carla and I belong to a group of gay men and lesbians in the Episcopal Church, Integrity, and we have found a lot of shy young people of both genders who are fearful of who they are and what they can become. Many are caught in the rigid prison of stereotypes and social role-playing, and many are dismally lonely. Jesus is there, in the midst of all of us, loving and embracing us all. Carla and I need each other and we need our God to be with us and in us. We both feel that we mean a lot more together than either of us could ever mean alone, and that is what we want to share with love and with integrity. That's our joy and our life. God loves us all.

Arnold's Story

I am a college professor, a church organist, husband of a disabled spouse, father of an adult son, member of Diocesan Council, member of the Vestry, a tithing Episcopalian--and a gay man. My sexual orientation neither adds nor detracts from the person I am; sexuality is merely one facet of my being. My wife and my son both know about me and love me anyway. I fervently hope that the rest of the world will be so understanding.

Gay people are still people. We strive for the same social acceptance the rest of the world wants. God made us the way we are--being gay is a *condition, not a choice.* Please love us as God loves us.

Nick Dowen's Story

I am a son of Ellen Barrett. We are all of us her sons and daughters.

Ellen's ordination to the priesthood on January 10, 1977, precipitated the events that brought me to Integrity for the first time. I probably could count on the fingers of one hand the number of meetings I have missed since.

I had never heard Ellen Barrett's name until I saw a fleeting television image of Bishop Moore ducking into the Church of the Holy Apostles to ordain her. He looked very uncomfortable in the glare of powerful bright lights and media scrutiny.

I paid little attention to this event at the time. Isn't it nice, I thought, that they would give our Episcopal Church some publicity! (In a city where Roman Catholics and Jews regularly dominate headlines it's hard to think that other religious bodies count for much.)

I soon learned that other people felt quite strongly about it. The Integrity/New York service just following Ellen's ordination was attended by over 400 people, still a record. This took place at the Church of the Ascension on lower Fifth Avenue, where Integrity was then meeting.

Ascension's vestry, of which I was a member, reacted quickly. At our meeting following this service, the vestry voted to ask Integrity to leave. The rector, one other man, and I dissented. Three people! I felt sick, frozen by a bitter arctic frost. To have one's own true nature voted against! I felt I had an inkling of how the Jews in Nazi Germany must have felt. I felt dirty, ashamed, less than human. In a democratic country the majority vote has an absolute, irrevocable power; it seems a judgment without appeal.

When Martin Luther King, Jr., had appeared in the news, my aunt and uncle from New Orleans said, "Black people as individuals are really very nice, but their organization into groups is something to be hated and feared." At the time theirs seemed to me a strange, inconsistent, and illogical opinion. Why do people feel so threatened by groups? I wondered. Now I think I know: it's because an individual can easily be defeated, while a group is strong.

Following that fateful vestry meeting I had all I could do to get myself home and telephone my parents. I needed to feel in touch with the attitudes and values that had molded me, decent American values like cordiality, hospitality, giving everybody a chance, allowing groups to assemble freely. I was born and raised in Montana, and I pitted our clean values against those of the wicked, decadent and deceitful East. People from "back East," my father used to say contemptuously, expect you to take them hunting in a blue serge suit!

I found the wonderful emotional outlet of attending Integrity meetings, in June, 1977, just after the chapter came to the Church of St. Luke in the Fields.

My interest in the Church of the Ascension steadily declined. I was able to pretend for a long while that nothing had happened. Like many other gay people, I am pretty good at concealing my own true feelings, sometimes even from myself. But the day came when I would enter the Church of the Ascension and see, instead of the John La Farge painting of the Ascension of our Lord, the image of the vestry seated in an upstairs room voting Integrity out. Instead of the Louis Saint-Gauden angels carved above the altar, I would see the image of the wardens of the vestry leading their fellows to perform a vicious act.

It was the end of my youth.

Luis's Story

Stop Praying to God for Miracles Now!!!

I managed to live most of my life without hope, never knowing exactly what it was, although having a vague notion that it had something to do with old Puerto Rican ladies who would always sigh and look at the sky and exclaim, "¡Qué lucha!...Tienes que tener esperanza" ("What a struggle, but you've got to have hope."). I always dismissed the saying as simply peculiar idiosyncratic behavior of old immigrant women. Sadly, hope, who might have been a good friend, was cast aside to be forgotten along with Catholicism, machismo, heterosexuality, and family. Like many lesbians and gay men of my generation I left behind all reminders in the neighborhoods we had grown up in: the Lorain, Ohios; the Islip, Long Islands; the Macon, Georgias; the Jamaicas, Queens; and the Boise, Idahos. And we came to Camelot with a dream of being new people: new men and women unencumbered by the baggage of our previous lives. It all seemed to work because we created a beautiful world that finally made us happy. It was a world in which there was little to struggle for, little to hope for, because it was all there just for the taking, because there existed an abundance of what was. You didn't ever hope, you just assumed there would be more tomorrow.

On occasion I would receive visits from my old childhood friends that I thought I had left behind -- the residue of a rigid Catholic upbringing, remnants of macho conditioning, and my family with all their blabbering about hope. They would always return eager to remind me of a past I had left behind. I accepted this as simply what had to be -- part of an unspoken bargain which had to be fulfilled without any understanding. My life continued rather effortlessly. It was essentially a charmed life. I was economically self-sufficient, I had a home I was renovating in Jersey City, my career was exciting and fulfilling, and I had a wonderful man to share my life with -- Dennis.

Then in October 1986, I discovered I had AIDS. As much as I knew about AIDS I realized just how little you know about it until you're diagnosed. You see, there is first: aids, an affliction of the body. Next there is: AIDS, an affliction of the spirit which slowly destroys the spirit both of you and of those who love you. It was the latter which I learned late needed to be ministered to because it was the latter which was "Killing the Dream" and leaving me with nothing more than despair. Understand that often those things which give our lives meaning come from "Things"; yes, things from the world out there. When something like AIDS disconnects the flow, we are left with an inner poverty which is profoundly hard to heal.

The year 1987 was a tumultuous year of coming to grips with life. For me it was even more specific than that; it was coming to grips with the notion that it was the end of a life. You see, AIDS poses many dilemmas which one must act upon. In my case it was not contemplating the inevitability of death. No, I was dying. We all knew that. I had lost 30 pounds, was incontinent, couldn't walk, and was in horrendous pain which only morphine could take away. Finally my vital signs started to give way and I received what amounted to final rites from my priest.

In the hospital, desperately scrambling to make meaning of those few precious hours and days which I might have left, I did everything which one imagines one does at this time. I said good-bye to friends, I told my lover I loved him, and said "I'm sorry" to my mother (I thought about it and realized that if you're going to die on a Puerto Rican mother you must say, "I'm sorry"). I did all I was supposed to do and lay back to await what was to come...and, you know, nothing happened -- no white light, no tunnels, no new age meditative music -- NOTHING. Then, one of those "pain in the ass" friends from childhood came to visit. It was my old friend hope, complete with her Spanish accent. Hope brought with her fond memories of those old Puerto Rican ladies who went on about the struggle of life and the importance of hope. Then, I understood. *Hope does exist and it exists in one's belief that you can live, that you want to live, and that you'll do anything to keep on living.* Hope helped me realize that I *am not doomed.* When we concede to fear and hopelessness we are, in fact, doomed. When we insist on living and surviving and when we do what we can to heal both the body and the spirit, we are not doomed.

I've learned one thing. The key to dealing with AIDS is self-healing -- that is, healing myself despite what may happen to the physical body. Hope allows me to confront my brokenness and heal it so I can be ready. Hope brings with it acceptance. Acceptance of what's so. When we deny, we exclude our brokenness; and when we accept, we include it and become whole. This surrender to God and to the illness produces a wonderful gift: serenity. We achieve serenity when we arrive at a balance.

Although I now know that life is essentially tragic, unjust, and unfair; that despite all the love and support, you are alone; that you cannot escape from ultimate pain and death; and that you are ultimately responsible for your life. I still maintain hope.

You can look at it in either of two ways: You can experience it as the end of the dream, or you can look at it as the fulfillment of life and love. I've stopped praying to God for miracles now; the real miracle is inside you, if only you would use it.

(Acknowledgment is made to Paul Reed for his helpful book, *Serenity*, published by Celestial Arts Press, Berkeley, California, 1987.)

Editor's note: *Luis Palacios-Jimenez, a member of Integrity/New York, delivered this sermon to Integrity/New York at the Church of St. Luke in the Fields on Thursday, February 4, 1988. Luis died in June 1989. He is survived by his lover, Dennis Costa, a former President of Integrity/New York.*

A clinical social worker by training and profession, with extensive experience in drug rehabilitation counseling, Luis was employed full-time designing AIDS education materials for the AIDS Division of Narcotics and Drug Research, Inc., a private corporation under contract to New York State. He served as a member of the Board of Directors of AIDS Resource Center.

Sheila's Story

To be like all my friends, I printed my boyfriend's name on the outside of my notebook and somehow knew to hide the name of my female "crush" inside.

It just "grew like Topsy," naturally, no matter how hard I fought it. I did not perversely *choose* to love other women. As far back as I can remember, I adored my school teachers, Sunday School teachers, and certain older girls. I pretended one after another was my mother. (I had a mother, but we were not at all close.)

These feelings gradually became more intense and confusing. Other girls didn't seem to have them, and I sensed that I shouldn't talk with anyone about them. In high school I first heard the word *homosexual*, but it sounded so dirty and sinful that it did not relate to the idealized feelings which led me to write poetry and bicycle by a teacher's house in the moonlight, yearning for a glimpse of her. I dated boys but felt guilty at any heavy kissing and felt so scared when one would mention marriage that I would drop him.

Finally, in my sophomore year of college, I had to face the fact that my love for a senior woman included sexual feelings. We were active in church, Bible study, and student missions; and I felt intense guilt at not being able to overcome my feelings. After many agonizing tears, sincere prayers and "re-dedications" of my life to Christ, my despair led to hospitalization for a suicide attempt, the first of many to come over the years.

My dear preacher-father was summoned to see about me and assured me that God would give me victory over this "sinful" inclination. My male psychology teacher (who touched my breasts when he had me hypnotized once!) advised that whenever I was tempted I should back up several yards from a telephone pole, lower my head, and run with all my might into the pole.

I entered medical school to become a missionary doctor, but the turmoil of the struggle against my feelings for that first college love, who had moved to the same city, was too great. I gave up medical school, left that love and that city, entered graduate school, and prayed desperately for a man. A very macho one came along and I quit just short of the Ph.D. to move to his town to marry him. He turned out to be homosexual, however, and broke our engagement.

I was soon in guilt-ridden and tormented relationship with a woman who also had become my dearest friend. We were active in church work and struggled against the sexual aspect of our love, always hiding it and seeking to overcome it. How I grieve that my guilt did not let me stay with her! After several self-destructive incidents--like crashing my car through a brick wall--I left her and a teaching position to attend seminary, determined to "overcome my sin" and become a missionary.

Again I prayed for a man and think I fell in love with one dear young seminary student; but a simultaneous "crush" on a "mother-figure" caused such inner conflict that I again became suicidal. I was hospitalized and given many electroconvulsive and insulin shock treatments. I then "vegetated" on anti-psychotic drugs in and out of hospitals for about one and one-half years until one psychiatrist who believed in hypnosis and in my intelligence taught me self-hypnosis to get me off the medication. Praise God!

The second miracle was being hired on a weekend pass from a state mental hospital to teach college again. After a struggle to get on my feet, interact with people, remember my subject matter (after the shock treatments), and stand before classes, my third "love" came along. Again, we were active in church work, felt intense guilt, fought our sexual feelings, and hid our love from all. Still convinced that same-sex love was wrong, I was often suicidal and sometimes even violent against her in my guilt and frustration. Still in psychotherapy trying to change my inclination, I finally got her "married off" and then got married myself.

I so wanted to be "normal" and to have children, but I was in for a surprise because my husband had not told me that he had had a vasectomy! He had lied about many things--having a college degree, having no debts, etc. Nevertheless, I had meant my marriage vows and I gave him everything he wanted--sexually and financially, but he left and I never saw him again.

I was devastated. I cried out to God to help, and a voice in my head said clearly, "Help yourself." I returned to school to change my field and get the Ph.D. in psychology. I had not been able to overcome my love for women as a "sin"; perhaps I could cure it as a "mental illness."

Graduate school in psychology was the beginning of many more years of trying to understand myself and change my basic nature. I tried every theory and therapy available and, in my intense longing to be heterosexual, even let one charismatic therapist seduce me. This was the only man I'd "known" besides my sterile husband, and I got pregnant that one time! I couldn't understand why God would keep letting these things happen to me when I was trying so hard to go "straight." Devastated and suicidal again, I opted for an abortion, for which I carry a profound sorrow, even though I believe I did what was best in my circumstances.

I was still so determined to love men that I underwent the best that psychology has been able to offer--aversion therapy/orgasmic reorientation. As is usual with this approach, I was worse off than ever! I now would get nauseated attempting to make love with a woman and could only be satisfied physically by a man, yet emotional intimacy and bonding were still possible only with a woman! (Fortunately, most of the results of this "therapy" tend to wear off after a few years!)

For years I let myself associate only with heterosexuals; and despite all efforts to resist, I became attracted to a straight woman friend. She had become curious to experience a woman's love, but then she ended our friendship of many years.

Devastated once more, I became celibate for seven long years. During this time, a straight woman whom I had befriended in many ways for two years, always sublimating my love for her in generous friendship with no "strings" attached, suddenly dropped and even snubbed me. At age 50, I was broken-hearted and felt doomed to a hermit's life without even heterosexual friends.

The AIDS crisis was in the news, and I was dumbfounded to hear many so-called Christians saying it was God's punishment, in apparent ignorance of its being a heterosexual phenomenon elsewhere and in ignorance of lesbians' low risk for it. AIDS correlates more with promiscuity than with sexual orientation. The church may have contributed to gay promiscuity by not blessing and supporting same-sex unions. I began to think that I might have to "come out of the closet" to stand up with my "brothers" even if I were celibate the rest of my life.

A month after turning 50, I attended a lecture on homosexuality and AIDS for a college gay organization and learned that several callers had threatened to bomb the building! The so-called Christians turned out in force, disrupting the meeting, waving their Bibles, and telling the young gay men they were going to hell. The latter were much more Christian in their behavior than the "Christians"! They patiently requested the Bible-thumpers to let them finish the meeting and graciously offered to sit down and listen to their point of view afterward. I was profoundly moved.

That night a campus minister gave me a copy of the chapter "What Does the Bible Say?" from the book *Is the Homosexual My Neighbor?* It condenses and simplifies some of the research of scholars like John Boswell (*Christianity, Social Tolerance, and Homosexuality*). It explains all of the Biblical passages. I came home and read it and made a list of the agony I'd put myself through: suicide attempts, hospitalizations, years of extreme "therapy", sacrificing MD, PhD, and seminary degrees, giving up my three loves, going through career changes, divorce, abortion, celibacy, rejection by friends, etc. I decided it was SIN for me to continue to put myself through such anguish and to reject and try to change the way God has made me. In the few years since, I've finally known peace, after half a century of struggle!

In God's great synchronicity, the next day I "happened" to attend a retreat led by a friar who "happened" to be gay and who shared his story with me. He celebrated the way God had made him. The priest who serves as my spiritual director also supported me, and she suggested that I become active in Integrity, which has provided blessed comfort and support. My parish priest had preached against homosexuality, but I shared my story with him and his wife when he was elected a suffragan bishop. Although they gave me warm hugs, they did not support my position. My parish and community are very conservative, and my colleagues in psychology can be quite unenlightened and prejudiced. I believe my loving father sees things from heaven's perspective now and rejoices with me. My mother has known since my college days that I was trying to change or abstain. About a year and a half ago, I told her as lovingly as I could what I had realized almost four years earlier. She remains extremely upset. I grieve over that, having hoped that she would understand the new scholarship on the scriptures and rejoice over my peace of mind. I see it as an opportunity to love her more fully, however, and to grow in my dependence on God.

I do feel at peace for the first time in my life. I desire neither to "flaunt" my sexuality nor to be ostracized. I do want, however, to share my experience when it might help others be at peace about their own or their loved ones' experience and to love themselves and others more fully. My vow is still to remain celibate unless God provides a life partner. In such an event, I would rejoice if my church would bless our commitment publicly and support our love openly and allow us to share God's love with others without hypocrisy.

First Ralph's Story

Old cats were once kittens. I've been an Episcopalian for over forty years, coming into the Church in college. Now I'm 62 and so a senior citizen, I guess. I went through the Navy in WW II and then to college still not knowing anyone else who was gay. I came out only in seminary.

Discovering that there was a gay community (Yes, Virginia, there was one even in 1950), I needed to sort things out. I went to NYC for the summer to work and make money to continue seminary. I stayed for the following 36 years. I retired early a year ago and moved to the "country."

Active in a parish from the time I arrived in New York City, I served at the altar, cooked church suppers, and became a vestryman and warden. Early on I had a gay family in the parish, including many active men and a few lesbians in the parish over the years. Some joked that we had the oldest servers and the youngest vestry for a city parish. I am sure that any who stayed in the parish for any length of time knew that many were gay, yet no one mentioned the fact.

Sometimes after Sunday Mass, six to ten of us would get together to have breakfast and to visit, and occasionally to read aloud parts of a new gay novel. Many gay couples were thought of as just that, however, you might want to explain it. We thought of them as we spoke of them: as "Tom and Dick" in the same breath -- no explanation. Three or four couples from this group have now been together over 30 years. Ours was a supportive association.

I never lived in a closet, really. If asked, I told. Only two or three straights ever asked, but each time I felt great. I was never openly out of the closet either.

After 25 years, I began to attend Integrity/New York enjoying worship with those who are gay, know it, and know that I am. The strong bond of love means a great deal to me.

For a few years I was out of the city on Sundays, and when I attended church there again, I went to St. Lukes in the Fields, where Integrity meets. At the time a gay men's group met sporadically, and I agreed to host the group. For a couple of weeks someone announced at the coffee hour that the gay men's group would meet at my home. That announcement meant a great deal to me. It confirmed how I had been living since coming to New York City. I was now an announced Christian and an announced gay man. The whole parish knew and cared -- just cared.

Thomas Michael Thompson's Story: A Eulogy

by Frederick Nesetril

Tom didn't say much. I wasn't sure that he even wanted to talk to someone gay and Episcopalian, although he had requested to talk to someone like me through the hospital chaplaincy service at St. Vincent's. Something was going on in his silence that I did not decipher in that first meeting.

Tom had just seen the movie "Early Frost" on television and was quite upset. The drama portrays an upper middle-class family's problems in dealing with their son's diagnosis of AIDS and his admission of being gay.

Tom and I talked at length about how the movie did and did not relate to us and our families and to the realities of the AIDS crisis. We talked about the unfair and cruel disease that Tom had come down with. We talked about some of the good and bad times that we had had in our lives as gay men. We talked about our love/hate relationship with organized religion. We eventually talked about everything, and I found out that Tom's ability to talk was sometimes greater than my capacity to keep up.

Tom wasn't sure he wanted to tell his family about his diagnosis at that time. There were too many compelling reasons not to tell them. One of his sisters was battling cancer, and he didn't want them to have to deal with another illness. Also, he didn't want his gayness and its connection with AIDS to drive any more wedges between his relationships with his mother, father, sisters and brother. At first Tom felt he would not die from AIDS and chose to keep his illness a secret from his family. As his illness progressed, however, Tom became aware of its finality. Eventually he visited his family, thinking it might be the last time he would see them while he still had some good health left. But, when he came back from the visit, he had a large hurt inside that, like the AIDS, never quite healed.

In time, Tom had a good amount of openness about being gay, about recovering as an alcoholic and living with AIDS. This openness came from Tom's acceptance of his illnesses and from his tenacious vision to make the best out of who he was and what he was dealing with. He wrote biographical articles for the PWA Coalition Newsline and for Holy Apostles News. He once told me he felt compelled to write about himself because of the tremendous bigotry, ignorance, and fear that people have about AIDS, alcoholism and about gay people. And Tom not only wrote about but also lived a life that spoke chapters about his bravery and ability to confront ignorance, bigotry, and fear.

For a while if Tom met someone for the first time, he began "the routine," as we jokingly called it. "Hello, my name is Tom...I'm gay, alcoholic and have AIDS." He could pull it off in one breath. When he used these counter-tact routines, it was not to drive people away, but to give them the opportunity to deal directly with him. Many people didn't understand that about Tom.

Tom often attended an AA group, PWA group and church group or service, one right after another. He was pushing himself to get all the help that he could, in a non-stop approach that kept him in touch with many, many people in one day. He communicated much of this drive to all the people he encountered. For example, he had to be hospitalized many times during his illnesses, so he became adept at the handling emergency room. He knew when to plead and when to scream. Even though he might be suffering, he knew how and when to deal with often overworked emergency room people. Tom also became close to many people in AA and PWA Coalition and Gay Men's Health Crisis.

Tom liked to hike, to go out for a movie or to a Broadway play. Tom liked hugs the most; he constantly hugged many of his friends.

Tom had a deep love for his church family at Holy Apostles. I am sure that much of the love that he had for his own family got transferred to us. At times he questioned the sanity of his church family, to be sure. He regularly attended healing services here and made it a point to transfer his membership so that "I can feel like I am more a part of all of this crazy place." We used to refer to it jokingly as "Holy Impossibles." He even made fun of me for my extreme love of smells and bells liturgy. But, if Tom didn't get scheduled as an acolyte for a while, he would let Cary or one of us know in no uncertain terms that he didn't like being passed over. When we scheduled him to "serve Mass," as he put it, he took his job seriously and with his own self-assured ease and grace in some of the most complicated services and human situations here. As an usher, Tom would welcome people at the door with that broad grin and escort them to a pew with a warm politeness and hospitality. Sometimes he walked them home to their doorsteps after a late meeting.

Even while his health faded, Tom also did some volunteer work in the soup kitchen, and later in the church office. He used to enjoy the soup kitchen work, especially, because "I was on the other side of that line before, and I know how it is for us when we have to be on that line," he once said. Tom identified with the downtrodden, the hungry, the sick, the poor, the needy. He was probably more of a Christian than many of us in this respect, because he had a deep understanding of the underside of life.

Tom took on many activities in his short stay with us in this parish. Some of them he accomplished, and some of them he did not. But, Tom's warm grin and hugs remain for us a symbol of what Tom was about.

Getting back to that silence that I said I couldn't decipher when I first met Tom, I think I'm beginning to comprehend what it was about. He and I were arguing about something one day, either something he didn't want left in his will or left out of the memorial service. All of a sudden I noticed that silence again, that something that was going on in his head that I wasn't a part of. Was he really that angry, I thought? He didn't look angry, just silent, somewhere where I wasn't. Finally, I asked him what he was thinking about. He said nothing. I knew he heard me. It was as if he weren't here in this world. When I looked more deeply at him, it suddenly occurred to me what Tom was doing. He was praying not from a book or a memorized prayer, but without words, without thoughts; quiet, deep within, not a hush, not a sigh, simply praying.

Tom's smiles and hugs were also prayers. So, let's not forget Tom's smiles, his hugs, his praying. When we pray, let us pray with smiles and hugs, too.

That's probably what Tom is doing right now. He's probably praying for all of us. I know it now because I knew it then. Tom is simply praying. For all of us.

Kurt's Story

After the military, I went to an excellent school with high academic standards and was invited to join a prestigious social fraternity. I loved the school, the study, the discussions, the parties and the fraternity. I loved it all. Life looked good, so good, in fact, I "pinned" a pretty girl. Yet, it was not right.

I tried a lot, worried a lot, and yes, prayed a lot. It wasn't that I'd actually had homosexual experience; in fact, I'd had no sexual experience of any kind. The realization came well before the deed.

My earliest recollections of life are Christian recollections. I became involved with the Episcopal Church as an adult, because I could sing. While a young soldier, I was confirmed at St. Mark's Episcopal Church--one of the happiest days of my life.

I have often failed in my youthful commitment. Yet, Christ has always brought me back, representing to me a God far more agreeable than some seem to imagine.

Many have loved me and supported me just as God made me. They have given me joy, and I love them and remember them. I am tempted to feel that others have failed me and have misunderstood me. If they have, I can forgive them and love them.

I believe that God is far more gracious, loving and forgiving than we sometimes see God to be. We are heirs to the same eternal plan as are all our brothers and sisters who share our common humanity. "O Lord, in thee have I trusted: Let me never be confounded." (Te Deum laudamus)

First Peter's Story

I hid. "Let no one discover my difference," I vowed. I spent all my childhood and my early adult life trying to "fit in." I felt my survival depended on hiding.

As the oldest of five children in my family, I have lived in Tucson since I was 3 years old. About that age I realized I was different. I didn't know the name for it, but I knew my difference was not "right."

My family certainly did not discuss homosexuality, but my parents taught us that bad habits can be overcome if you work at overcoming them. We believed that failure to break a bad habit resulted from laziness.

At school I felt lonely and miserable -- always an outsider. I spent so much energy on guilt that I set myself up for failure. My pain interfered with my scholastic and social skills. So far as I knew, no one else in the world had this differentness.

As puberty approached, I learned colorful names for my difference (*faggot - fairy - queer - sissy*). I feared others would use these words to describe me, so I worked even harder to smother my sexual identity.

I believed what society taught me: Queers are evil, worthless and hated by God. My good feelings were bad; my dreams were bad; I was bad. I felt I could change if I never admitted to others that I was gay. All would dislike me if they knew I was queer. So I hid. I skillfully made my mask, a straight self, behind which I hoped I could somehow destroy the my gay part and be normal. Worst of all, I participated in ridiculing other gay people so everyone would think I was straight.

People never discussed sex at church, even at my Episcopal Church. One time I tried to bring up the subject with the rector of my parish. He looked like he would die of embarrassment. Years later, that same priest physically prevented representatives of Integrity from attending a Eucharist at our parish.

So I invested in the "American Plan." I fell in love with and married a woman. I tried for nearly ten years to be straight. The lowest point of my life was when my hope and illusion of being normal began to fall apart, as did my family. I was tired of trying to be something I was not, and I began to dread the prospect of the long, weary years ahead trying to maintain the deception, with no prospect of ever being myself. It became increasingly difficult to deny my feelings and eventually it became impossible to resist being who I am.

I was enraged that God would allow me, his child, to feel intense conflict over feelings which came naturally.

Finally I decided to share my problem with my new rector. I felt my life was over, but anything was better than the hell my insides had become and the hell my family was beginning to feel. After I finished coming out to him, he asked what I wanted to do about the situation, so he would know how to help. I shall always be grateful for the love, support, and healing that he offered me on that evening.

During other sessions with the priest, I began to discern that *normal* differs for each person. I began to hope that God had intended for me to be gay. I was not bad by nature.

My life has altered radically, and I am grateful for the love and support of my gay friends, Christian and non-Christian. A few friends and family members could not cope with my revelations. Others have nurtured me, and I thank God for them.

I have loved the same man for nearly five years, and last October he and I exchanged vows in a Blessing of our Union. It was a beautiful experience for everyone who witnessed it.

When younger, I felt that being gay manifested weakness. I believed that sexual orientation was changeable. By the time I came out, I resigned myself to my orientation as a given, inexorable. I now believe that I despaired over my sexual orientation only because society pressured me to do so. Sexual orientation is as involuntary as skin color or national origin. I believe God gave me my orientation, and surely God would grieve if I tried to be any other way.

I am attending college and hope someday to be a counselor working especially with gay youths on issues of self-esteem and coming out. I pray that my church, the Episcopal Church, will become more vocal and active in the support of gay rights.

I do not ask to be tolerated. Tolerance is for bad weather and rush-hour traffic and chest colds.

Gay people are dying from beatings, from harassment, from self-hatred, from AIDS. Homophobia is as deadly as AIDS. The Church's failure to repent is as evil as the fag-bashers' hatred, guns, knives, and stones. I celebrate all God's children and encourage our wholeness.

John Andrews' Story

My Uncle Bob and Aunt Madge Andrews used to be notoriously stingy about Christmas presents, and their Christmas present to me one year in the 70's was their last three issues of *Book Digest* -- a monthly magazine which consists of condensations or excerpts from six or eight current best-sellers.

I was a badly overworked graduate student at the time; but the following summer, I finally found time to begin reading those *Book Digests*. As luck would have it (I think it was more than luck), one issue featured a selection from Laura Z. Hobson's *Consenting Adult* -- a first-rate novel about a family coming to terms with having a gay son, made into an equally first-rate TV movie. (Its author was the sister-in-law of the late Bishop Henry Hobson of Southern Ohio.)

Early in the book the gay son, Jeff, reflects on his inner life and feelings:

> Pete [Jeff's roommate] was always carrying on about some girl he was in love with, slobbering over what he had done to her and everything he was going to try next time. Jeff hated hearing it, but he half memorized Pete's words, as if he might want to borrow them for his own use. The thing was, he never knew exactly what Pete meant, knew it in his head, sure, but not really knew, the way you know things you actually did know. He listened to all that about kissing and feeling and trying to do this or that, but it was like being locked behind a wall of thick glass where you could see out but not get near anything yourself.

He didn't know exactly when he had first realized that. He only knew that whenever he
read a book with a big love scene or saw a
movie with passion and breasts and open lips,
he had that same dead lost feeling of being
locked behind that wall of thick cold glass.....

As I read that passage, I realized, "You know, that's ex
actly what it's like for me." Something inside my head
went "click," and I knew. At last, at the age of twenty-
four, I knew.

It took me years to begin accepting it, because I also
"knew" that all homosexuals were deeply and sadly disturbed people; I "knew" that homosexuality was the
lowest, most unmentionable, most reprehensible of
sins; I "knew" it was just impossible to be a good Christian and be homosexual.

The church played a crucial role in pulling me out of
the vortex of self-hatred which that "knowledge"
plunged me into. I attended an annual Province V
campus ministry conference, a conference devoted to
issues of sexuality and spirituality. Then, gradually, I
began to discover my own university chapel congregation to be welcoming, accepting, and supportive. I can
hardly tell you how much that church and its people
came to mean to me as I continued through the com-
ing-out process.

My good friend Jim is now an Episcopalian and a
member of my campus parish, partly as a result of our
friendship. When I found the courage to tell Jim I was
in love with him -- and found that he wasn't gay (which
isn't to say he didn't love me in other ways) -- it was the

support of our chaplain and other friends in the congregation that helped us both through the difficult period that followed. I think that we could not still be closest of friends if we had lacked the support of Christians in that community.

A couple of years later I met CF, my first lover, at the chapel. Our joy enlarged by our not having to hide our love. We could share it with our friends at the chapel and know that it brought joy to them, too. Later, when CF left me - completely without warning -- the chapel community again saw me through. Jim held my head in his lap while I cried for a good half-hour. Paul and Patty, a graduate-student couple, took me into their home for a week or so -- and they hadn't even known I was gay before this happened, but, in the fashion typical of our chapel, that didn't make a shred of difference to them.

Last fall one of the bishops of our church addressed his brother bishops at their meeting near Chicago: "Ask lesbians and gay male Christians to tell you how the Church has made them feel, not what the Church says about them, but how the church makes them feel. No one will tell you that the Church has made them feel loved. Analyzed, yes. Allowed, sometimes. But not loved."

I rejoiced to say to that bishop, "I'm writing to tell you precisely that. The Church has made me feel deeply loved as a gay person -- specifically, the campus chapel congregation to which I belonged for nine years while simultaneously finishing my PhD and inching my way out of the closet." I went on to tell him: "What keeps me going to Integrity is the fact that in that congregation, I have been to the mountaintop, and seen and known what the Church can be to gay and lesbian people when it has its act together. The point, of course, is that every congregation ought to be that sort of place, and far too few are."

Not long before his death, TJ and I had spent the evening together in his apartment -- not making love, but just stretched out on TJ's bed holding and caressing. Afterward I came back to my room to go to bed and began my devotions, which generally start with the Lord's Prayer. This particular Lord's Prayer was the strongest of my entire Christian life, a cross between prayer and meditation. After each clause of the prayer, I reviewed its implications. The whole experience lasted, I suppose, fifteen or twenty minutes; and at the end I somehow knew that the peace I felt with God, and the peace I had just felt with TJ, were really one and the same peace.

Dottie's Story

While my friends were in love with Clark Gable, I was in love with Doris Day. I remember how hurt and angry I was when I realized in my late teens that others accepted it as normal to change plans made with a girl friend if a male date appeared.

I had grown up in an ordinary middle class Presbyterian family and participated fully in all the children and youth oriented activities of the church through high school. In retrospect, I can see a pattern of close friendships with girl friends and intense crushes on women.

Living in a dorm during my college years gave me ample opportunity to compare my life with that of other women. To my friends, dating was the first priority; to me it was something I did to be part of the group.

At the end of my sophomore year I met Gil, the woman who was to become my partner. From the beginning I knew that I wanted to share my life with her. I did not want to admit to myself what that meant. Over the next few years the desire to be with her did not go away. I knew no one who was homosexual. Probably, I didn't even know it was possible for a woman to be one. But I did know that society in general and the church in particular frowned on the idea. Worst of all, I feared that any discussion of the subject would drive Gil away.

During most of our early years of friendship, we were separated by thousands of miles which gave me ample time for reading and prayers. Reading proved to be disconcerting. Textbooks portrayed homosexuals as psychologically ill. The Bible saw homosexuals as abominations. The few writers who even bothered to mention lesbians typically described us as tough and masculine. While I saw myself as strong and independent, I was comfortable with my femininity.

Prayer served better than reading.

Gil was an Episcopalian. I started attending Episcopal services. I knew that on the other side of this country, Gil was in church listening to the same lessons as I was. I was confirmed as an Episcopalian and continued to spend hours in church seeking an answer. God speaks to us all in mysterious ways. Gil was living on the West Side of New York. While I saw *The West Side Story*, the song "There's a Place for Us" gave me the courage to pursue my dream.

Six years after our meeting, we became lovers. The struggle to find who I was ended.

Within our hearts we knew this was right for us, but society had taught our friends, our employers, and our church not to consider it right. We kept our love a secret, as a way to survive. Initially I was uneasy in church when I said the prayer of confession. "We have followed too much the devices and desires of our own hearts. We have offended against Thy Holy Laws. We have left undone those things we ought to have done and we have done those things that we ought not to have done; and there is no health in us." As our love for each other and for our church increased, it became clear to us that we *were* doing what we ought to do, and the health *was* in us!

In the late 1960s we became active in a church in San Francisco that was inclusive and socially active. I had my first taste of what it means to be part of the Family of God, part of the Body of Christ. I longed to be honest with that family. My need to be honest with our congregation intensified when Gil underwent surgery for breast cancer. I faced the day of surgery alone, denying myself the comfort of friends out of fear that I would reveal the true nature of our relationship. The loneliness overwhelmed me.

Soon after Gil's surgery we made a Cursillo. One of the spiritual directors was the deacon of our church. Having sensed our conflict, she included these words in one of her talks: "God's gift of sexuality shared in mutual love with due regards to our responsibilities to both the community and to each other--any gift thus shared in thanksgiving to God who gave it, is well used. There is no small print about being married, or over 18, or of a particular sex. No other unbreakable rules."

At last I felt free to break my silence and seek her counsel. We discovered that the congregation had known we were a couple for years. Rather than seeing us as a liability, they saw a stable lesbian couple as a resource. The church became our only safe space. Any remaining conflicts between sexuality and spirituality were gone.

Within a few years we moved to a small town in northern California. We knew we were taking a step backwards in openness, but we also felt we were being called to share the joy of the Christian community we had experienced in San Francisco. For seven years we assisted in developing a Cursillo community, increasing lay involvement in liturgy and creating a sense of family in our new congregation.

When a new rector came, he described himself as a "strong anglo-catholic with a capital C." The phrase put fear in my heart. Eventually he called me into his office and asked if my relationship with Gil was sexual. When I said yes, he announced that he had spoken with the bishop and then read a disciplinary rubric from the Book of Common Prayer: "If the priest knows that a person who is living a notoriously evil life intends to come to communion, the priest shall speak to that person privately, and tell her that she may not come to the Holy Table until she has given clear proof of repentance and amendment of life." He was asking me to confess the love that Gil and I had shared for the past nineteen years as sin! When I refused, he suggested that we find a "lesser church." Somehow I managed to hug the man and tell him that I felt sorry for him. I left his office determined never to enter that church again.

After an evening discussion and tears with Gil, and a fretful night's sleep, I awoke with a clear vision of a friend who had also experienced rejection in that congregation. She was walking proudly down the aisle of the church. I had a strong sense that we were being di rected to do the same. I wrote to the rector stating that we would not come to the rail without his permission, but we would not be leaving. "We are part of this family. Families should not reject members when they do not approve of their behavior but should pull together to work out the differences." I was confident that Gil and I could demonstrate that our relationship was a Christian union.

For the next two years we remained in our pew during communion. Christmas and Easter found us in unfamiliar churches because the pain was too great. We no longer served as lay readers, chalice bearers or choir members. With few exceptions the town's seemingly conservative congregation loved and supported us. We had polite but restrained conversations with the rector. The bishop agreed that the priest had the right to follow his own conscience on the matter but demonstrated his own belief by giving us communion on his visitations. We frequently returned to our San Francisco congregation to receive its love and Communion. Members of Integrity, the Parsonage, the Cursillo community, and friends from all over the country, some of whom we have never met, sent messages of support. In many ways this was one of the most positive experiences of our lives. When Gil retired, we left that church and moved on to another community. The rector had not changed his mind.....nor had we.

People have asked us to describe our feelings during that period. I could never find the words that fully express the emotions. Soon after his election as Presiding Bishop, I heard Edmond Browning expand on his statement "there will be no outcasts in our church." He said, "To many people the church has proven to be a broken promise." That was it! The pain of being denied communion was a broken promise.

In August 1990, Gil and I celebrated our twenty-fifth anniversary. It has been quite a journey: our love for each other and for our faith has deepened. With the help of many Christian friends we have changed from an isolated couple quietly attending church to a couple who feel called to devote our energies to assure that "in *our* church, there will be no outcasts." Today our ministry is to share the Good News that God loves us, gay or straight, and to assist the church community to keep its promise to *all* of God's children.

Barry Levis's Story

I knew sometime during first grade. I could not play dodge ball as well or run as fast. I tended to stay off by myself. My mother used to blame the fact that I did not go to Kindergarten. All I knew was that I was awkward and often alone.

I did develop a good friendship with Bill who moved next door that year, and throughout school we remained chums. But most of the other kids in my class did not befriend me. Only Marvin, the one black boy in my class, associated with me. I was not, however, permitted to go to his house, although for a long time I did not quite understand why. My parents discouraged me from associating with anyone who was different, perhaps the reason I came to reject myself.

I had an otherwise very loving mother, although not the close confining type that homosexual males are supposed to have. My father came from the old school. I know that he loved me, but he believed in strong discipline and very little affection. I think he really did not understand me. Both my older brothers had more in common with him; they became engineers and not teachers. My brothers always said I, being considerably younger than they, had been a "mistake."

I was not a happy child. In particular, I hated gym class because of the humiliation involved with it. I always played left field in baseball, and if there were more than one of us there I always was sent out as far as possible. Increasingly, I retreated into my own imagination, living in a world that was often much more real to me than what I had to experience at school. Never among the group of popular children, I became a constant target of the bullies because I could not defend myself. One boy took delight in lying in wait for me after school every day to take out his vengeance. Therefore, I spent much of my free time in my room reading books and listening to classical music.

We went every Sunday to the Tioga Baptist Church in Philadelphia, where my parents had met and been married. It was a long drive from the suburbs where we lived, but they did not want to break the ties with the church where most of my relatives went. One of my grandmother's sisters was a nun in the Episcopal Church and the other served as organist at St. James the Less Episcopal Church. Yet everyone else in the family was Baptist, and my father regarded his Episcopal aunt as an embarrassment. I never thought much about being a Baptist. Like all of my church peers, I was baptized when I was twelve; but mostly I fought with one female cousin, who invariably beat me up. I later learned that she is a lesbian.

My sexual awakening came quite by accident. Mother did not reveal the facts of life until she gave me a book when I was seventeen. Actually a boy named Brentwood had already opened my world of sexual pleasure under the train platform in my attic. While playing hide and seek, he introduced me to an even more pleasant game which took me quite by surprise. From that day on I became addicted to it. My attic became quite a meeting place for many different boys. My mother often went out in the afternoons, and even when she returned she did not bother us. We all became adept at dressing quickly and quietly when needed. Throughout junior high we carried on although one by one, the group dwindled. Names like *fairy* and *queer* became associated with our activities, and the fear of discovery became too intense for some. Nevertheless, I enjoyed the game so much that I continued long after many of the others had quit until I too became worried about labels. By that point Bill and I remained habitués in the attic. One day I announced that I had outgrown it when Bill indicated his interest in a frolic. It was very hard for me to walk into my house alone that day.

I have trouble pinpointing when my interest in girls arose. Actually my interest in boys never ended. I was intrigued with them even when I was very young. During the summer at the shore, I watched the men shower next door. Only the middle portion of their torso was hidden by the wooden door of the outdoor shower; I watched intently to see if I could glimpse what the door concealed. I also played with Ginny in the back seat of my parents' Pontiac. She would show me her thing and I would show her mine. I remember thinking how lucky I was to have what I had. Much more attractive I thought. Yet I became involved with girls in junior high like my peers. In fact I was spending afternoons with Bill in the attic when I first went steady with Janet. From that point on, I was never without a steady girl-friend for long. Yet I know that I was more intrigued with the boys than the girls. I remember admiring Tim Considine on the Hardy Boys series and closely emulating his dress and characteristics. Today I would call it a boyhood crush. Later in high school I had a similar reaction to the student president. I even cleaned my glasses every morning the same way he did. Perhaps I thought I would begin to look like he did as well.

When I went off to college, things did not change much. I got pinned three different times. I also joined a fraternity which had a large shower room where I could often get a peek at the forbidden organ. By this point I began to worry that I was homosexual. I had heard that boys normally went through a period of experimentation but later outgrew it. I, however, found myself still strongly attracted to men. I did not fall out of my chair every time a beautiful woman appeared on television. The first time I saw a Playboy I was disappointed that I did not react the way my friends did, although I made a good pretense of it. All through school the boys made comments about me, often intimating that I was a "fairy." I tried to prove my masculinity by telling tales of my sexual exploits, many of them invented. One of my penmates, however, did assure my brothers that I functioned quite appropriately. I felt relieved.

My religious pilgrimage by this time was well underway. I had left my parents' Baptist church in high school to attend one closer to home, mainly because Bill and many of my friends went there. I also switched because I did not find the other service stimulating. My first exposure to Anglicanism came when I was on my high school senior trip to Bermuda. On Palm Sunday, a group of us went to the Anglican Cathedral in Hamilton. I spent the entire service trying to figure out where we were in the Prayer Book and felt rather silly having to kiss the palm cross before the priest presented it to me. Yet somehow that experience had smitten me.

When I got to college, I stopped going to church altogether for several years. At times I professed to be an atheist, a position fashionably correct in the early sixties. My undergraduate major was biology so that I had to give appropriately scientific explanations for the universe. Somehow they just never sounded right coming out of my mouth; I always had a sense of unease, perhaps that same sense I felt when I protested my heterosexuality. Like Descartes, I doubted; but finally I arrived at a point beyond which doubt would not carry me. Slowly I began with an understanding of God which looked nothing like what I had accepted rather blindly as a child. God became a figure of love rather than sternness; he ceased being the judgmental Father, like my own, and became the creator of a marvelous universe full of mystery and intricacy. He just might, I thought, have enjoyed immensely the process of creation. My study of biology revealed the great complexity of nature. I could not believe that it had all come about by chance. An unfathomed intelligence must have put the pieces together. Moreover, I sensed a tremendous joy in that creation that lay beyond the superficial harshness and cruelty of nature which had always put me off. I came to understand that God loved all that he had created.

Nevertheless, God could not as yet love a homosexual.

I played with these religious ideas but did not set foot into a church. I knew that I could never be a Baptist again. These new thoughts had other profound impacts on me. I began to move away from science. I had only gone into that major because it seemed respectable to my father. I knew I could not major in engineering like my brothers; I had absolutely no interest in it. Yet my true love, history seemed impractical.... Although I completed my biology major, I announced to my family that I was going to graduate school to study history. My stern father was flabbergasted but my heavenly one seemed to approve. For the first time in my life I followed that inner voice, my intuition, rather than cold calculation or pure reason. I also began slowly to alter my politics. I had been active in the Young Americans for Freedom and enthusiastically supported the

Goldwater campaign. Yet somehow these ideas began to ring hollow. I paid lip service to the intensifying war in Vietnam as long as my student deferment continued. Later when I registered as a Democrat, my father accused me of being a Communist.

I began attending church again with a fraternity brother, Sandy. I now realize I had fallen in love with him; it certainly was much more powerful than a simple crush. I hung around him as much as possible and even began going to church with him. Although an Episcopalian, he dated a Methodist; and we attended her church. Sandy insisted on kneeling during the prayers, and I followed suit. I enjoyed kneeling, but the service came too close to the Baptists for me. I knew that I did not want to become a Methodist. Every once in a while his girlfriend Bev would condescend to attend the Episcopal church, and there Sandy revealed the mysteries of the Prayer Book to me. For the first time, I began to immerse myself in the beauty of the liturgy and the symbolism which I found as intriguingly complex as the structure of the universe. Surely God was talking to me here. By this time, I had entered graduate school and took a course on Reformation history. I think Henry VIII clinched it for me. I knew I had to become an Episcopalian, and within a year Bishop DeWitt of Pennsylvania confirmed me.

About the same time I met my future wife Pat. I had been dating another girl for several years, but it just didn't seem to click. Pat came from my home town, although I did not know her until we met at college since she was several years younger than I. She came from the right side of the tracks, her family lived very comfortably, and my mother approved of her as much as she would approve of any prospective wife for one of her sons. It seemed a match made in heaven. Yet it took me three years to ask her. There were a number of things wrong which created a sense of unease. At one point we broke up because of constant bickering between us. In the end, I decided that marriage to her would be easier than trying to find another. I ignored the inner voice that kept saying no.

I continued to look at men but thought it was only a passing phase. I had not done anything since I was fifteen and thought it was gradually going away. Nevertheless, one month before my wedding, my attractions confronted me in an alarming way. I had taken a summer job at a Philadelphia department store. One of my coworkers was getting married on the same day I was, and we often talked about our respective plans. One day she came over to me. "Barry, if I didn't know better, I would swear you were homosexual."

I must have reeled with horror at hearing those words aimed at me. "Why did you say that?" I sputtered.

"It's the way you look at men. You don't look much at the women when they enter the department, but you look the men over very carefully."

From then on until the day I got married I scrutinized the women entering the department with special care. I also realized how difficult it was not to look at the men. On the night before the wedding, Pat knew something disturbed me. That inner voice of mine practically screamed no. I worried about whether I really wanted to spend the rest of my life with someone who was not always very pleasant. I also brooded about those feelings which just would not disappear. Nevertheless, we got married the next day in a grand Episcopal fashion. Pat had been raised Presbyterian, only because it was the closest church to her house. Her religious sense was never particularly strong, and I had insisted that she become an Episcopalian. I know she did it under protest, and throughout our marriage she never shared my religious enthusiasm. Eventually she practically ceased going to church at all, and following the divorce she stopped entirely.

Following the wedding we went to England for a year so that I could complete my dissertation. I had gained an interest in church history and had decided to do my work on eighteenth-century England. The time in England was rather peaceful, but upon our return my dark side began to emerge. While doing research in Philadelphia I stumbled upon a bookstore which specialized in gay pornography. To this day I will never know how I managed to enter the door. That first time I stayed but a few minutes and fled in horror. I returned later, however, and took a longer look at the material and the literature. Several years later I mustered the courage to enter the movie theater attached to the store. I remember how filthy the place was and how filthy I felt when I left. I surmised the strange things occurring around me; but I strictly focused my attention to the screen, where I was riveted by the entirely new world opening to me.

Shortly thereafter my first son was born. I had resisted having children for the longest time and especially feared a son. After all, weren't most homosexuals child molesters? What if I turned out to be one also? During the pregnancy the homosexual fantasies began in earnest. I had been bothered with them before; but now they came with regularity, as if they had a life of

113

their own. We had moved to Florida and had become communicants at the Cathedral Church of St. Luke. The guilt associated with these fantasies and the rare occasions when I would attend one of those movies when I was out of town drove me constantly to the altar rail to light a candle and pray desperately that God remove these unnatural desires from me. He didn't. In fact they only became worse. Next I thought it necessary to confess these sins, but of course I could not do that at the Cathedral. I had to wait until I was on sabbatical in England to go to confession there. I slipped that phrase about unnatural sexual desires into the midst of a long confession hoping that the priest wouldn't notice. He did but explained that as long as I did not act upon them I did not have to worry. I hadn't and had the most exhilarating feeling after it was over. I had turned out not to be a child molester either, and this time I pressed for a second child, also a son.

Yet the urges still did not dissipate. They became more insistent and overwhelming. At the same time my wife became increasingly uninterested in sex. Our relations had never been particularly satisfying; but now she became too absorbed in the children to have much time for me. I was left to my inner thoughts. Not until I turned forty though did I decide I had to act on them. I came close several times when I was out of town, but I could never get up the nerve even when I had a very clear offer. I was going on sabbatical again to England, however, and thought that there, thousands of miles from home, my chance might come. I knew I could not preserve my sanity if I did not do something. I had become a man possessed. The more I prayed, the more powerful the urges became. Anger and frustration began to come between me and my faith. No one was listening. Was anyone there?

When I arrived in London, I began to search out the haunts of homosexuals during my lunch breaks from the British Library. Within a short time I had discovered a pub called the Golden Lion, which I later learned catered mainly to hustlers or, as the English call them, rent boys. The first time I entered the pub an attractive young man heavily cruised me. I instantly fled. It took some time before I gained the nerve to return. I finally became acquainted with the young man, and we would often talk. (I, of course, used an assumed name.) He invited me to meet him some evening, but I always had an excuse: I had a wife and two children at home. Eventually, he disappeared and I never saw him again. To this day, I do not know if he was actually a hustler or not. Desperately hoping to meet him again, I continued to inhabit the Golden Lion. No one else there actually interested me, and I waited anxiously for his return. For some reason, as I left the pub each day, I would hum Bach's "Sheep may safely graze." It became as compelling to me as my desire to find a sexual outlet. I even began to hum it at home, so much so that my youngest son memorized the melody himself and would ask why I hummed it so often.

My efforts to encounter that young man again came to naught. Finally I began exploring some of the other pubs, but by this point I had almost given up hope of finding anyone. About three weeks before our return to America, I entered the Salisbury, a pub in the theater district which catered to both straights and gays. There I met Brian. When I entered the pub, I noticed him almost immediately. He was talking with another gentleman, but he soon started to return my gaze. (I had gained a certain proficiency at this technique since my first time in a pub.) How we ended up at his flat is too long and torturous a story. I finally had tasted the forbidden fruit, and it devastated me. I later told friends it was like being picked up and thrown against a wall. It had been a rather rushed experience at that since I was meeting my family for dinner and a show. Recently I saw Starlight Express again since I do not remember the first thing about the performance that night.

I got to see Brian once more before I had to return to America. The flight home was one of the saddest times I had ever experienced. I had no idea what I would do with myself at this point. I returned to the Cathedral with a heavy heart. I had cheated on my wife and had my entire life turned upside down. That Sunday the choir sang "Sheep may safely graze." I could not keep the tears away. I knew that a message of hope existed there. Yet for the next six months I was in a deep depression. The Bach tune was often on my lips, haunting and persistent. I could not explain to anyone what bothered me. I thought about going to a counselor or one of the priests in the church, but I feared they would ridicule me. I prayed constantly that these desires, now burning within me, would vanish. They progressively grew more demanding. Relations with my wife slowly came to an end, but (I thought) I could not identify any gay persons in Orlando and did not know where to locate them.

Finally, I met someone in the choir who went to London as often as I did. My suspicions about him proved quite correct: we patronized the same pubs. We had a short fling, but he soon tired of someone who could only see him occasionally under the strictest secrecy. When he dropped me, I again panicked. This time, however, I finally broke down and talked with a friend from the Cathedral. Earlier, during my period of depression, I had mentioned to her my extreme anger with God. I explained that I had asked Him repeatedly for something, and He had not answered my prayer. At that time, she suggested He actually had, but I just did not understand yet. Now I confessed to her the reason for all the resentment and hurt I felt. My life came gushing out. She practically ordered me to see one of the priests at the Cathedral and actually made the appointment for me.

When the canon and I met for lunch, he did not laugh. It became my first step toward recovery and self-acceptance. We had several long conversations, and eventually at his urging I undertook counseling. She in turn encouraged me above all to follow the inner voice I had failed to obey so often in the past. Shortly after our first conversation, I attended a convention in Washington and worshiped at the National Cathedral. Again I prayed fervently about what I should do with my life. The choir sang "Sheep may safely graze" for the offertory. I finally recognized God's voice consoling me.

Within a year I had told my wife, and eventually we divorced. The end of the marriage caused great pain to many people. The scandal deeply wounded my former wife, and it disrupted the lives of my children. If I had only listened to that inner voice, I might have spared them the grief. At the same time, I am grateful I have children. They are a source of great joy and I believe that despite the trauma they have become stronger and more resilient, self-accepting and tolerant of difference in others.

About the time of the divorce, I met the man with whom I hope to spend the rest of my life. I am now openly gay to my children; in fact the eldest chose to live with Mark and me, and my youngest son calls Mark his second dad. I am also open at my college where I have Mark's picture on my desk. Finally, I am open at church. Yes, some are disturbed about what has happened and object to my presence. For the most part, however, I find acceptance and understanding there. Even my (now former) bishop embraced Mark and me, and wondered in bemusement why the Episcopal church attracted so many gay men. I remain very active in the Cathedral and serve in a variety of liturgical and educational functions. I hope my example will help some come to terms with their own homosexuality and aid others in understanding that being gay is not a curse from God but His gift. The Shepherd loves all His flock. It took me a long time to comprehend that, and I suppose it will take many others at least as long. We must have patience, love, and perseverance.

Christian's Story

I almost didn't go in when I wandered into St. Luke's Church on Hudson Street in February 1988. I'd been away from the Roman branch of the Holy Catholic Church for more than 7 years.

When I was young, I became smitten with the idea that I should be a Roman Catholic Priest. I 'said Mass,' mumbling the Latin words just like the monsignor did on Sunday. I became a 'disciple' of the pastor, accompanying him on his walks every afternoon and absorbing Catholicism from him. I was young, after all. Many small children felt that priests in their robes and hats with pom poms were exotic, something holy, other than ourselves.

At the same time I began to feel a pull towards expressing love toward my own sex. The monsignor would have been horrified, I suppose. I adopted the attitudes of my family and my priest -- I denied my attractions and subsisted on solitary moments of pleasure thinking about the guys in gym class or the underwear ads in the Sears catalog. (Yes, repressed gay boys really do peruse the catalogs!)

So, religion and adolescence blended for me into one horrible mess. I was holier than everybody else (or so I considered myself), and became an insufferable prig, shunned by those whom I secretly admired. I still had the vision of myself saying my first Mass in my home parish, admired by all. Except myself.

I came to New York City to go to Columbia, still an insufferable prig. Although many avenues of pleasure were open to a gay teenager in New York City, I was still convinced that I would burn forever if I satisfied my longings. I also was convinced that as a future priest I would make myself impure by giving in. So I didn't.

After graduating from Columbia, I applied to a seminary in Boston, and was rejected. Rightly. I was still insufferable, 'demanding' admission to what I had come to see as my destiny. I returned to New York and bitterly worked to be admitted to a seminary here. I had to prove that I could do it, after all.

I was admitted to a seminary, worked hard, and still denied my sexuality. However, in the seminary every man was supposed to deny his sexuality. I felt right at home.

After 2½ years, I left because I was no longer an insufferable prig. One thing the seminary had done for me -- it had taken my faith away and replaced it with nothing. Religion was a business in the seminary. We were to celebrate Mass everyday, hear confessions every Saturday, make the rounds of the hospitals, associate only with other priests, keep custody of the eyes. I felt like a doughnut -- the middle of my soul was taken out and sold like a Munchkin in Dunkin' Donuts.

So, I left and pursued a career. That hole was still there. I finally stopped denying my sexuality. But I'd begun denying my spirituality. It seemed that I couldn't have my sexuality and my spirituality at the same time. Once I'd lost the other, I'd gain the one.

I had always been attracted intellectually to the Episcopal Church. During my time at Columbia I was a regular communicant at the Cathedral of St. John the Divine. However, I now wasn't about to surrender to any Church which would make me deny my sexuality again.

Then, last February I found Integrity. That first Eucharist was a cleansing experience. I had never before worshiped with people for whom sexuality and love integrated with spirituality. My eyes began to tear at the Communion hymn. I had filled the hole, bought back the Munchkin. I was back on track. Although I thought I had lost faith, I gained back something more. I now could begin believing that Jesus loved me. He loved me as I am, not as I could never be, after all.

I have now joined the faith community at the Church of the Holy Apostles, where I can attend faithfully and proudly as a gay man among gay men, lesbians, straight people, blacks, whites, women, men, all on that same road to really believing that Jesus loves us, all of us. He encourages us to realize our total soul, our entire being. Our destiny is unity with God, whatever road we take to get to God. And, there are many roads, after all. I will be received into the Anglican Communion on October 2nd, God willing.

And, I now know that, after this life is over, God will welcome me just as I am. I pray that, while I am still here, my sisters and brothers in the Episcopal Church will welcome me, just as I am.

Daniel's Story

The phone woke us very early on Saturday morning. Paul answered it, mumbled something and handed it to me. We had been expecting a call anytime. Dad had been fighting cancer for over a year, first one kind, then another, and finally a third. So I was somewhat prepared when I heard Mom say in a tired but peaceful voice, "Daniel, your father died about half an hour ago." Even so, I could manage only a weak "OK" in response. I don't remember the rest of that conversation. What I do remember is Paul's holding me and rocking me in his arms as I hung up the phone and started to cry. It was the first of many times over the next few days when I would turn to him for comfort and solace.

Only a few hours later, Paul and I were on a plane, headed for Mother's home in Ashtabula, Ohio. Beforehand we hectically prepared. We bought airline tickets; arranged for a friend to watch the house and the cat; did our laundry; packed and rushed off to the airport. The time on the plane was our first chance to pause and take stock. I was sad, mostly. Dad was gone. There was a hole in my life that would never be filled again. I was also relieved. Dad was finally at rest after a long struggle. I was even happy. My family was all gathering for the first time in more than a year. With forty of us (counting brothers, sisters, spouses, nieces and nephews) spread over so many states, we cannot get together often. Despite the sad occasion, I looked forward to being with everyone.

I was also anxious. This was the first time Paul was going with me. Fortunately, most of my family had already met him on trips through Atlanta over the past several years. So the awkwardness of the initial introductions was behind us. Still, I was anxious. To meet and accept Paul on our 'turf' was one thing. To receive him as another in-law in the very heart of the family homestead was something else again.

In the first few moments after we arrived, Paul faded into the background with the other in-laws, as I shared a tearful reunion with my mother and the others who had arrived before us. However, that private circle soon opened to include the wider family and Paul was swept up in a love that made no distinctions. And the embrace of that love continued for the rest of our stay. During that time, everyone made a point to spend some time getting to know Paul better. The warmth of their welcome heartened me for it told me that they recognized Paul's importance to me.

It was a wonderful visit. Our family reunions are more like family re-creations. There are too many new faces and too many changes to the old ones to be the same family. So we create a new one each time. This re-creation was better than most, for we had longer together. Usually, we rush in for a wedding and scatter almost as fast with hardly a moment to spare for visiting. This time was different. Dad had died Friday night. By Saturday evening we were gathered. In fact, since calling hours would not be until Monday, we had an entire day, Sunday, to ourselves. We didn't even have to worry about food, for a constant stream of neighbors and friends bearing covered dishes kept us well supplied.

With that many people together in one home for such a long time, especially when a good number of them are young children, and with a constant flow of food, it does not take long for a relaxed informality to set in. We lapsed into occasional zaniness. At one point late on Sunday afternoon, with more food in the house than even we, forty-two strong, could handle, another car pulled up. As these new visitors got out of the car carrying flowers, an irreverent cheer went up. "Good, it's flowers! We don't have to eat flowers."

Paul and I found ourselves wrapped up in the warmth of being at home. Yet we were never as comfortable as the others. How should we carry ourselves during this time? Like most lesbian or gay couples, we adjust our displays of affection radically depending on the circumstances. In our own home and those of our close friends, we sit close together, touch often, and may even exchange a quick kiss. In public, however, we are constantly on guard, restricting our actions to knowing glances or stealing a quick touch only when we are sure others are not looking. How should we act among my family?

I was probably more uncomfortable than Paul. It's always been easy for me to share with my family the fact of my being gay but difficult to share the emotions under the surface. Maybe I try to protect them from what I imagine they do not want to know. At any rate, it was not easy for me to change gears on this visit even though I was with Paul. Mostly through my manipulation, we settled into a way of interacting that was closer to our public than our private norm. In fact, at one point Paul complained that we were being so distant that the others were likely to conclude we did not really care for each other.

Perhaps Paul was right. At one point, one brother-in-law did refer to Paul as my "buddy." Although he meant no harm, it hurt. I wanted to shout at him, "We are not buddies. We love each other. We share our lives. We have committed our lives to each other just as much as you and my sister have. We are lovers, spouses, mates." But I remained silent. I did, however, resolve to show a little more open affection for Paul.

The most unsettling moments came when someone outside the immediate family was there. My mother is still "in the closet" as a parent of a gay man with her friends, and my aunts, uncles, and cousins. When her friends were there, Paul and I tried to make ourselves scarce. When that was impossible, Mom gracefully introduced everyone using first names only. She dropped the relationships (for example, 'and this is Paul's wife Pat') that she normally provides. This did not work with my relatives. Since they stayed longer and expected to visit with me, there was no way that Paul and I could simply disappear. In this case, we couldn't get by with the simple trick of introducing people by first names. To them, a newcomer like Paul stands out. So, my brothers and sisters introduced Paul variously as my "friend from Atlanta" or my "roommate."

Playing this game of make-believe with Mom's friends was not bad. I do not know them well and do not want to share my life story with them. Besides, Mom had enough on her mind at the time without the added stress of 'coming out' to her friends. But playing this game with my cousins did hurt a little. How can I expect them to share anything important about themselves? Especially Steve, who is in his late teens and, I believe, gay. What does he think when I say nothing? Does he understand why I am silent? Or has my silence made his own coming out all the more difficult? I do not know. Maybe next time.

It could be worse. I used to play make-believe all the time -- at home, at work, and at play. One by one, I've broken out of those chains and released the truth. I am richer for the experience, and so are my family, my friends, and those I work with. Some day, this final barrier in my family will also fall. Again, we will be another measure richer.

It is a similar hope that keeps me in the church. Yes, there are people in the church who hate gay and lesbian people and work to exclude us. Others merely tolerate us while wishing in their hearts that we would go away. Yet, I have hope. As I have seen my family, friends, and co-workers grow and change, so have I seen a few in the church accept gay and lesbian communicants with open and loving arms. Some day, more will follow their example. We will all be that much richer.

First Gary's Story

I was reared in the Church with a positive view of God as loving yet firm, not a god of fire, brimstone, and inescapable punishment. My understanding of God and the Christian faith developed rapidly at the same time as the awareness of my sexuality became clearer. At the age of eighteen, I confronted the realization that I was truly gay and was not merely going through a phase. My belief that God loved and accepted me did not waver, and this assurance helped me get through that traumatic period. I knew in my heart that God cherished me, and as my sexuality was a core element in my identity, then God must cherish my sexuality too.

The realization that I was gay did not affect my relationship with God, but strained my ties with the Church and my family. God seems not to be too concerned with what society thinks. I have kept reminding myself that the Church and my family receive the news of my homosexuality in the context of their cultural biases.

The topic of my gay orientation is not open for discussion with my family; it is one of those skeletons that came out of the closet. The familiar reaction is to ignore the issue in the futile hope that the "problem" will go away. Since my immediate family refuses to deal constructively with my sexual orientation, I withhold much of my life from them. I do not share people and events important to me. Sadly, those who nurtured me as a child and a youth miss out on my continuing, personal evolution. I am growing and developing as an individual, yet my loved ones see only a small picture of who I am. We all lose.

My relationship with the Church has also suffered somewhat. I have considered myself to be a child of God, yet have questioned whether I belong in the Church. I have lived in different parts of the country these past several years and have tried to judge the social and spiritual climate before revealing my personal nature to others in the local Episcopal church. My experiences have ranged from total acceptance to absolute rejection. The Church is supposed to be the family of God, and like all families, I have found areas of friction within it.

I often brace myself emotionally when I mingle among other congregants since I do not know what to expect if others find out that I am gay. Sometimes they accept me just for being Gary, sometimes as a curious oddity, or as a "nice young man," and at times they greet me with nervousness or hostility. I find it easy to handle most receptions, yet I hurt when someone with whom I had been chatting during coffee freezes and refuses to have to talk further once the person recognizes my orientation. I keep telling myself that the good outweighs the bad, but rejection based upon something I cannot change often pierces me to my heart.

I don't understand why some think that I threaten the sanctity of the Episcopal Church, especially since I look upon myself as a person of faith. I am familiar with the Pauline epistles that contain a few negative passages about homosexuality, but I still cannot fathom the depths of people's emotions when confronted with this issue. I am who I am, and I certainly do not look upon myself as some vile creature bent upon destroying the foundation of the church. When I lived in Houston the relationship between the diocesan leadership and its gay communicants was deteriorating. I decided that since the leaders did not want me to participate I would remain on the periphery. I found myself in a lose-lose situation with the local church and did not like that.

Many changes occurred when I moved to Atlanta. After distancing myself from the church for a few years, I found a place that accepted me. Within All Saints, I have found an oasis where I can relax and not face rejection from the clergy or laity.

As I have witnessed by living in different regions of the country, the view of homosexuality varies greatly among dioceses and parishes. The acceptance I find at All Saints means a great deal to me, though I wonder how easily things could be turned upside down with changes within the parish or diocesan leadership. The lack of formal recognition within the Episcopal Church leaves me with a feeling of uncertainty -- will I become an integrated participant or a sidelined observer from a rejected subculture?

I try to stand back and analyze the issues and look at them from a historical, theological perspective. Yet when I, a gay man, am the subject of discussion, I become emotionally as well as intellectually involved. I realize that I am a child of God and much more than a mere theological specimen for the bishops to examine with passing curiosity. God is my god; the Church is my church; and though I might believe that I have God's blessing, I would also like to have the formal blessing and acceptance of the Episcopal Church. At the very least, I would like to have the Church respect me in my predicament; I am a gay Episcopalian who did not choose his sexual orientation and who wants to be accepted for being himself. God help us all.

Sandy's Story

Jesus loves me, this I know,
For the Bible tells me so...

I have loved this hymn all my life. It confirms that God loves me. During my late teens and early twenties it was especially comforting because I did not love myself. In fact, I hated myself most of the time, believing that I was total filth, not because of anything I did, but because of who I was.

Raised as a devout medium-low Anglican, I experienced a strong evangelical influence. My maternal grandmother was Baptist, and my mother was with the Brethren before she married. The oft-repeated penitential elements of the Book of Common Prayer deeply affected me.

At seventeen I became involved with a fundamentalist Protestant youth group. They drilled into me that I was unworthy, that even my best was worthless. God could not tolerate imperfection, and only the Blood of the Lamb could atone for my sin. Quite orthodox as far as it goes. However, accepting their emphasis on self-degradation I failed to perceive and value the incredible magnitude of the mercy of God.

I also bought into the distorted theory of justification: God loves me only because God looks at me through Jesus-colored glasses. So God doesn't really love *me*, as I am unlovable. God loves Jesus, and I get filtered out. Certain about my orientation, I thought of it as a defect and did not act on it.

I prayed to be a different person, and God answered, as God often does, in a way I did not expect. In university, I attended a high Anglican parish, and in the second year I joined a Catholic charismatic group. I began to see that truth is not as simple as I had thought. I discovered that fundamentalism was not the only authentic Christian spirituality. Yet I felt required to claim healing for my homosexuality, as if it were a disease or a wicked choice. No one had known, but when I told them of my change, they all congratulated me. In reality, I experienced no change at all.

After three years at the university, I took two year's of training at an Anglican seminary. There I learned much Church history and theology, and started reading the scriptures more comprehensively. I truly felt called to ministry, but all the while I kept feeling more and more like a fraud. I could not accept that Jesus redeemed and sanctified all of me. He has not issued merely an "ADMIT ONE" ticket excluding the rest of what makes me who I am.

I am driven by the need to be whole and to integrate my life. For me it is essential to be authentic in whatever I believe and do. I experienced tremendous stress when I could not reconcile the differences between my orientation and what I believed my faith dictated. I blew a gasket. I had to leave the seminary after an immobilizing depression, including two suicide attempts.

God refused to let me go, although I wanted God to abandon me and let me be annihilated. I still remember how, when I had given in to despair, a solid conviction of God's persistence came over me.

I needed several years to grow again to rejoice in the knowledge of God's love. Part of the healing occurred when I came out to myself. That is, I had to accept my orientation toward members of my own gender. I had to acknowledge the way I am put together. My orientation is not a product of my volition. I could not choose whether to be gay or straight. I could choose only whether to be gay and sick or gay and healthy.

Now I celebrate my sexuality as a God's gift. I look at what the Bible really tells me: Jesus loves me! God is with me! God will never forsake me! The new commandment is to love one another as God has loved us.

A few special people in the Church have aided me enormously on my journey. Most helpful were a couple of organizations of gay and lesbian Christians and their friends--Integrity and Dignity. I continued with theological studies, but I do not seek ordination. Current definitions of the system exclude me. I will not hide or renounce my committed permanent relationship.

God is greater than I can imagine. I must constantly do God's will and make the most of the talents God has given me. If I do, God will make the most of what I offer and will not refuse me. When I fall, God is my redeemer, my strength, joy, comfort, and my guide.

When asked if he believed in infant baptism, Mark Twain answered, "Believe in it? Hell, I've seen it!" Just so, of course it is possible to be gay and Christian. I am. Others may attempt to disallow that God loves and cares for me, or may try to discredit my faith, but "I know whom I have believed and am persuaded that God is able to keep that which I have committed against that day" (2 Timothy 1:12b).

Michael's Story

l realized that l differed -- in some profound way -- from most of my male peers. This realization terrified me. l believed that my family and friends would reject me if they ever discovered my terrible secret. Early I resolved that I would tell no one about my sexuality.

I cannot remember a time when I did not believe in God, and from earliest childhood I had a sense that my Creator loved me. This feeling has never changed.

I became increasingly involved in the evangelical movement, throughout high school and college, because I felt that this was my only hope for change and heterosexual marriage. I'm not effeminate, so it wasn't difficult to pass as straight. More than once I made off-color "fag" jokes in front of my evangelical friends. Far better to be considered a little worldly than to be suspected of homosexual tendencies!

Finally I could live this lie no longer. After a period of deep depression I "came out" to my minister and a few other friends. Needless to say, I was extremely contrite. As I told them how much I hated being gay, there was no doubt of my sincerity. I can still remember the deep relief I felt when at last someone else knew about my hidden struggle.

These people expressed their concern for me, and soon I was in the chair of a Christian psychologist. I also began attending a group called "Homosexuals Anonymous Christian Fellowship." My minister assured me that God hates homosexual activity. He did not doubt that God would make me straight if I really wanted to be. That is definitely what I wanted!! The minister also assured me that if for some reason I didn't change, God would help me live a celibate and happy life.

In less than six months it became clear to me that I am gay, always will be, and that I by no means have the gift of celibacy. My need for human intimacy is far too strong for that option.

Discouragement washed over me again. Even my psychologist admitted that there was no realistic chance that I would ever become heterosexual. The reassurances that my minister and friends gave me seemed almost laughably shallow and naive.

Finally I searched for help outside of my church community. Thankfully, I was attending a large university with a supportive group of counselors. For the first time in my life I talked with someone (a nun, surprisingly enough!) who told me that I was fine just as I was, and that God didn't necessarily want me to change. She suggested that I contact the Integrity chapter that met in our city.

This was a tremendous turning point in my life. Soon I had made a new group of friends and was getting counseling from gay-supportive clergy. I had never imagined that so many people go through just what I went through! Many of the new gay people that I met were also Christians, which surprised me.

Finally my evangelical friends found out what I was doing. They were appalled that I would "expose myself to temptation" by associating with people who accepted their gayness and even rejoiced in it as a gift from God. I ended my involvement in the evangelical movement in the church. Nobody ever rejected me overtly, but their condescending and patronizing attitude quickly drove me away.

Two years have passed; I have had virtually no contact with my evangelical friends. Over time I became more of a "militant homosexual" (Mr. Falwell's term), to deal with the anger and hurt I felt over having lost so many close friends just because l told them I'm gay.

So now I have a new life. I am active in my Integrity chapter and attend a supportive parish. I have focused my evangelical zeal on helping other gays find the acceptance and happiness that l have found. I have even been able to enter into a monogamous relationship with a wonderful man; this experience has shown me that love and commitment are just as possible for gay people as they are for those who are straight.

When I was younger I dreamed of someday being ordained. I pushed this dream aside as I got older because I could not reconcile my faith and my homosexuality. It causes me great pain that the Episcopal Church still officially bars self affirmed, active gay men and lesbians from the ordained ministry. Nevertheless, I deeply believe that the Holy Spirit continues to lead the Church into all truth. I have much confidence that the Church will one day accept lesbians and gays as equals in the faith.

My hope is in God and in the future. I know God created me gay for a good reason and that God loves and accepts me just as I am. Perhaps someday my dream of ordination will be rekindled, and perhaps someday the Church will recognize and bless the relationship that I have with my partner. I wait expectantly and with much prayer for that day to arrive.

Second Peter's Story

After long and careful thought, I have decided to seek reception as a priest in the Episcopal Church.

I was ordained a Roman Catholic priest in the Dominican Order in 1966. I had entered the Dominican novitiate nearly seven years earlier, in August, 1960.

I think I always wanted to be a priest, although different things about the priesthood attracted me at different times. When I was a kid, it was the mystery of celebrating Mass; when I got older, and knew more about it, it was preaching that attracted me. The opportunity to proclaim the Gospel seemed to me -- and still seems to me -- a great privilege and an essential activity in the life of the Church. It was that emphasis on preaching that attracted me to the Dominicans. Their official name is Order of Preachers. So, in 1961, I began the normal course of philosophical and theological studies in the Dominican Order.

During this time I was generally happy, both as a Dominican and as a priest, and I was secure in my conviction that I had chosen the right way of life. By 1969, however, this began to change.

In 1968, I had been sent to Rome to pursue a doctorate in moral theology at the Dominicans' university, the Angelicum. There my conflicts began in earnest.

In the aftermath of Vatican II, I found it harder and harder to reconcile my conscience with the teachings of the Church, especially in the areas of human sexuality and ecclesiastical polity. Also, I became more and more convinced that in order to understand who I was and what I was meant to do, I would have to understand my own sexuality. Celibacy began to seem like a serious stumbling block to my development as a person.

By 1971, I had arrived at a kind of compromise: I would leave the priesthood, but remain a Roman Catholic. Still living in Rome, I petitioned the Holy See "to be reduced to the lay state." This was ultimately granted by Pope Paul VI on June 13, 1973. In the meantime, I found work as a teacher of English as a second language in a school for Russian Jewish emigrants on their way to the United States.

In order to stay actively involved with the Church in some concrete way, I joined a group that had been established by Dom Giovanni Franzone. (Franzone had shortly before been removed by the Vatican as abbot of St. Paul's Outside the Walls and had set up a community in a working-class district of Rome.)

During that time, I felt very much on the fringes of the Church, although I continued to think of myself as a Roman Catholic.

Gradually. this compromise proved unworkable. By the time I returned to New York in 1976, I no longer considered myself a Roman Catholic. I did, however, consider myself an openly gay man and I knew that, with or without the Church, that was a step in the right direction. For the first time, I felt able to explore my sexuality, and here I met my lover, David, with whom I have lived for the past ten years.

Still the problem of the Church continued. Merely departing from the Roman Church did not seem the answer. On the one hand, I was unable to consider myself a Catholic. On the other hand, I was unable to imagine a spiritual life outside the Church, and I knew I needed such a life. I also knew that the Anglican Communion was a logical alternative, but I had not yet come into concrete contact with it.

This contact began in September, 1982. I started to attend the Thursday evening Eucharists at St. Luke's sponsored by Integrity/New York. So, in a real sense, my path to the Episcopal Church came through Integrity.

My gradual "discovery" of the Episcopal Church has been one of the great blessings of my life. Within the Anglican Communion I have found everything I knew I needed and had a right to as a Christian: the sacraments, the Scriptures, community life, prayer, and a living continuity with the great tradition of Western Christianity into which I was born and which has always nurtured me. At the same time, I found that the stumbling blocks to Church membership were gone. I found a Church where power is shared, where freedom and mutual forbearance flourish alongside orthodoxy. I found a Church where human reason and common sense are honored, a Church where the Gospel is preached and where people are helped.

I became a member of St. Luke's last year and was formally received into the Episcopal Church in April of this year by Archbishop Clarke. After a long and sometimes painful journey, I felt I had come home.

The AIDS epidemic has also played an important part in my decision to return to the active priesthood in the Episcopal Church. Since 1981, I have seen the Episcopal Church respond to the AIDS epidemic with heroic leadership. Our own bishop, Paul Moore, has been a great role model for me.

I have seen our clergy, our lay people, and our institutions respond to the tragedy of AIDS with courage and compassion. The establishment of the AIDS Memorial and Fund at the Cathedral of St. John the Divine is one excellent example of how the Church is trying to help. (I chair the AIDS Memorial Committee, made up of representatives of Integrity/New York and of the Cathedral, which administers the Memorial and the Fund.) The Saturday evening dinner program for PWAs at St. Luke's is another example.

Gradually, I have come to the decision that I would also like to play a part in the Church's ministry to PWAs as a priest. But most of all, I would like to respond again to a calling I have felt my whole life: to be a preacher of the Gospel, to share the Good News with others, and I would like to do so as a priest of the Episcopal Church.

I seek your support in this endeavor and, with God's help, I will strive to be worthy of it. I would also like to express my gratitude to the Episcopal Church, to St. Luke's, and to Integrity, for having offered me a spiritual home.

Editor's note: *Peter Carey, a Director of Integrity/New York, wrote this essay on June 11, 1987 for the Ministries Committee of the Church of St. Lukes-in-the-Fields. The Committee accepted him as a candidate on December 18, 1987. On June 13, 1990 he became a priest of the Episcopal Church.*

Manuel's Story

All the priests reprimanded and condemned me. In my pre-teens during the 1930s and 40s I felt unworthy to be alive. This caused me much doubt, worry, pain, and sorrow, not to mention depression. I couldn't understand why I was not allowed to be myself.

Being gay is a gift from God. I wasn't having problems with "me"; I was having problems with the Church and society's attempts to restrict me from being who I am.

When I was 17, my confessor advised me to seek medical help and have male hormone shots to counteract my homosexuality. He said that I was trying to kill an elephant with a cork "pop-gun" when I should be using a rifle. Hormone shots would straighten me out.

That was the day that I left the Roman Catholic Church. After hearing this nonsense I felt angry and at a loss. I had no other choice but to leave.

Years later I discovered the Episcopal Church when I left San Antonio and moved to New York in 1958. I became a member of St. Mary the Virgin in New York City. It took many years of analysis to clear up my hang-ups.

Being a member of the Episcopal Church and Integrity/New York has greatly upgraded my self-esteem and self-worth.

May God continue to bless Integrity for all its good Christian Ministry within the gay community.

Joseph's Story

I prefer to work within the Church to promote unity, rather than to protest from outside.

I am 37 and live in San Diego with my mate Stephen. We have been together for 17 years. I work as an administrative assistant for the law review in a local law school. Steve manages the telecommunications department of a large typesetting company. He has a B.S. in psychology, and I have two years of college. Our combined income is about $40,000 per year.

I was born and reared in Washington D.C., in an Irish-Scottish-Italian family. I was raised as a Roman Catholic. My Scottish grandfather, who died when I was little, was a Presbyterian, I am told. He died of alcoholism. After his death, my Irish grandmother, his wife, lived with us.

I lived in a very happy home, by and large. Both parents were present. My mother, Eleanor, an Italian-American, stayed at home during most of the years, but when I was a teenager, she secured a part-time position as a drugstore cosmetics counter clerk. Grandmother was at home all the time. She cooked and baby-sat. She and I became very close. She was a devout Roman and because of her influence, Dad also was religious. I am also close to my brother, John, three years my senior, and I have a sister, Carolyn, now 20. All of us were educated entirely in Roman Catholic schools through the 12th grade. Ours was the legalistic, authoritarian Roman Catholic Church of the 1950s.

Of three children, I was the most religious. Until I reached 12, I wanted to be a priest or brother. I wanted to go to seminary high school and be a missionary.

Puberty changed my life tremendously, and it is only now, at 37, that I can being to reclaim some of the good parts of pre-puberty.

At 12 the physical changes hit me with much illness, including severe acne, foot cramps, pollen allergies, multiple colds, and pneumonia. I had insomnia and nightmares until I was about 17.

My parents gave me almost no information about sex. I went to the library and read. At an all-boys high school, I had two horrible years -- 1965 and 1966. Other boys made fun of me around the clock. I embarked on two years of therapy, which proved to be successful.

At the end of therapy, I began to realize I might be what people called a "homosexual." The next year I entered a secular university in D.C., and discovered the gay bars. This was 1969, just prior to the Stonewall riots in New York, seen as the beginning of gay liberation. I went to the bars every night and attended school every day. After 6 months, I met my first lover. Due to his alcoholism, we broke up violently a year later. Then I met Steve, my mate. He helped me through my breakup with my ex-lover and has been helping me ever since, as I help him.

I felt that maybe it was time to give up altogether on religion. I'd stopped going to confession and to Communion about 1968. I knew I would never be accepted as gay and a legitimate member of the Roman Catholic Church. Having sex with someone of the same sex is still a grievous sin in the Catholic Church today, regardless of the depth of commitment. I think this rigid anti-gay position keeps homosexual people from Our Lord and leaves many scars.

I got involved in counseling other gay people. With leftist politics I centered my life around gay liberation and women's issues in the early and mid 1970s. I used alcohol extensively at this time. Still young and naive, I was attacked by thieves five times in 1972 and 1973. I fought them off each time, however, and was never seriously injured. The reason for the attacks was hatred of gay people, for each time I was attacked I was leaving a gay bar late at night.

After my troubled adolescence, my breakup with my first lover, and my being mugged so many times, my self-hatred increased. I was in therapy for about six or seven years off and on. My health was not great--I never exercised and I smoked and drank a lot. I am also not proud of my moral judgment about intimate relationships during these years.

Steve and I moved to Seattle in 1975, and lived there for the next 9 years. I had three or four secretarial jobs, and Steve worked as a secretary and then moved into graphic arts. I progressed a lot in Seattle in many ways, and as I see it now, I began to move into active alcoholism and drug addiction. The intense period of addiction began in 1982. I've always been a quiet and shy person, but always felt excluded, unloved. I did not love myself for many years. Alcohol and cigarettes had always been my means of escape from my feelings of anger and self-hatred. But they were not enough. I discovered that by using drugs I could become a lively, entertaining, witty person. I began using drugs and alcohol every weekend.

The heavy drinking and drugging continued as we moved to San Diego in 1984. We had a fire and lost all our possessions. I contracted hepatitis and then pneumonia, and I was out of work for many months. Alcoholism is a progressive disease. I hit bottom and had to quit my job in 1986. My brother had quit drinking the year before and my best friend in Seattle had quit in 1984 and was in Alcoholics Anonymous (AA).

I joined AA a year and a half ago. AA has totally changed my life for the better. Early on, I accepted the Second Step of the Program--that there is a Power greater than myself and, miraculously, I knew that the God of my childhood is still there for me. I knew that just because I had substance abuse and "lower morality" earlier on in my adult life, with God's grace and with the help of his Church on earth, people *can* turn their lives around. We can become more responsible Christians. Even gays.

When I accepted God again in 1986, I knew that Christianity was what would work for me as a way of life. I have a formal, traditional side, and I felt that since I'd been so thoroughly trained in Roman Catholicism, I should move towards one of the mainline denominations. I cannot return to the Roman Church because the Pope is viewed as infallible and has stated many times that homosexual acts are sinful. I do not feel welcome in the Roman Catholic Church. I feel they do not allow individuals to express themselves as different and unique. I attended the mystical/New Age churches such as Unity and the Church of Religious Science. Many gays have been attracted to these denominations

144

because they have been accepting of us. Personally, I feel that they are worthwhile, but something is missing for me. I thought of going to other mainline denominations such as the Methodists or Presbyterians, and I began attending the Episcopal Church. I felt so much at home that I've never seen any reason to leave.

I believe that God answers my prayers every day in the name of our Lord Jesus Christ. I am relatively healthy in these years of the AIDS Crisis. That itself is a miracle, given the beating I gave my immune system for years. I have not taken a drink for a year and a half, and that is another miracle. My finances are intact and that is a miracle. I have a stable relationship, a loving family which accepts me just the way I am and I have a spiritual life which gives me satisfaction beyond measure. I express my gratitude to God every morning in my prayers.

In my diocese the Episcopal Community Services is ministering to the homeless and to AIDS patients. I immensely respect our Church. Its commitment to the vulnerable keeps me here.

I'm here, too, because our Presiding Bishop has asked all Episcopalians to be as inclusive as possible. While I do not agree with a fundamentalist approach or a conservative approach, I try to be as open as I can to the conservative members of my parish. The parish impressed me when the people warmly welcomed me at the door and at the coffee hour. Two church women "adopted" me right from the beginning, and I have felt included here ever since.

I am in the Episcopal Church because I want to worship with the community at large, not isolated in a "gay" church like MCC. I need heterosexual people in my life. I serve coffee at the coffee hour once every two months with two church women. Also, I am in a class on "Believing" every Sunday with about 15 heterosexuals.

In summary, I feel included here, and that's one reason I joined the Episcopal Church.

The current Bishop of San Diego, from what I hear, is at least somewhat homophobic. Our Diocesan Convention recently passed an anti-gay resolution, and it hurts. I made a conscious choice to be an Episcopalian only after many months of reflection, and now I am "being rejected." However, I choose not to leave in a huff. I love my new Church and plan to stay in my parish in a loving, open, compassionate, moral life. Thereby others will notice that gays contribute a lot. We have other gays reading the lesson at Holy Eucharist, saying prayers with the elderly in the Episcopal Home in San Diego, and serving at the altar. Educators and priests who happen to be gay--although not openly--teach classes in our diocese. My point is that we are *already* making a significant contribution.

I admire the Episcopal Church for recognizing the importance of the individual's conscience and the individual's personal relationship with God. We don't have a Pope who dictates the "truth" to us. We reason issues out in the context of tradition and with the help of God's grace at General Convention.

I am glad that General Convention has affirmed that homosexuals are children of God and entitled to the full love and pastoral concern of the church.

I believe that we need to lead a moral life, preferably

within the bounds of a committed relationship, participating in regular prayer, attending Church regularly, and receiving the sacraments. Aren't these the truly important aspects of Episcopal life?

Can persons born gay really choose who attracts them? I was born with this sexual orientation. With God's grace and with the help of the Church, I plan to lead a morally sound personal life. Also, I intend to continue to support our Church enthusiastically.

In their 1987 Pastoral Letter, the House of Bishops wrote, "We have faced on differing levels the reality of our prejudices. We continue the exciting but arduous task of dialogue between the way we understand our faith and the stunning explosion of contemporary knowledge." The Presiding Bishop said in the same letter:

"If one speaks of God's love but does not act out that love, or if one acts out that love without interpreting one's action, the fullness of our Gospel is violated.... I deeply believe that without justice there will be no peace, liberty, or equality. Justice is the ultimate good, grounded in our biblical heritage and patently demonstrated in Jesus' ministry. No society can be too just, no individual can act more justly than is good for him or her or for others in the society. The Church must be the first, not the last, to point out and protest instances or institutions of injustice; racism, sexism, elitism, classism are social heresies that also violate our covenant with God, making them theological heresies..."

Mayne's Story

I always shake my head when someone claims that gays and lesbians "choose to be that way" or are shaped by dysfunctional families. I consider myself living proof that such statements are lies. My parents' marriage was and is still the most stable, loving and mutually beneficial I have ever seen. I had a strong model for heterosexual womanhood in my mother, who was a capable, effective, dedicated wife and mother. My father is a uniformly good masculine influence--home every night and thought well of in the community. We wanted for nothing financially. I was the eldest, smart, doing well in school (though never popular), healthy, fit, and even rather pretty. And here I am, a lesbian.

I knew from the age of eleven that I was different. In my journals, I have found occasional agonized passages: "I can't seem to be able to join in, be like the other girls.... I wonder if I'm a lesbian?" Strange that I chose that word, which came closest to identifying what was different about me, despite my complete ignorance about lesbianness.

I wondered on through high school, which I remember through a hot haze, despite our temperate climate: a state of embarrassment, loneliness, awkward heterosexual fumbling. I clung to the vision of myself as a writer, because it did help explain why I didn't see life the way other girls did. When I was nineteen, I tried for the first time to talk to my mother about my embryonic lesbian awareness. Upset, she accused me of trying to frighten her. I understand her reactions now, but she scared me so badly I didn't let myself think about being gay for eight years.

Instead, I tried what some would call promiscuity -- though such a judgmental word is so relative that I won't generally use it in any context. Sexuality was always a serious issue for me. It seemed to be the only thing I had to assert against the nay-saying of religion, society, parents. What was called sexual freedom in the seventies was an insidious pressure, and heterosexuality, celibate or not, failed me consistently, despite my efforts. Still more difficult was the insistent pressure of God's voice. I can remember standing at the window of my apartment shouting aloud, "Leave me alone! Let me live my own life!"

I did turn to religion, hesitantly becoming involved with charismatic Christians, while one male ex-lover accused me of using it as an escape. He had, of course, his own reasons for resenting my choice. It was not an escape from, but a re-exploration of things I had felt without well understanding. Throughout the years of trying to conform to the world--a constant pressure for gays and lesbians as well as Christians--I knew Jesus was with me. It is hard to make this intelligible to people who refuse to believe a lesbian or a gay man can be a Christian. I always knew Jesus as a constant loving presence. Sometimes he and I did not communicate well, but I knew this worried him as much as it did me.

From my professed Christian friends I did not get much guidance or help about leading a Christian life: only that one did not have sex outside of marriage (gayness wasn't even mentioned), or swear, or drink, or smoke, or --if you were a woman -- criticize men.

To be honest, I did not much like many of the professed Christians I met in my twenties. They did not tolerate anything they did not approve of. Part of my rebellion, despite the token outward conformity I could muster, had to do with my feminism: I wanted not to turn into a pious canting female, like many Christian women I was getting to know, who had no pre-marital sexual feelings and were either intellectual snobs or openly anti-intellectual. I also rebelled to protect my writer's gift: otherwise I might stop writing what I needed to write and write only devotional material.

Still isolated, searching, feeling like a fraud at the gatherings I attended, in my second year of university (I began at 21, not 18), I met a professed Christian 13 years my senior, who had NOT sacrificed his intellect to dogmatism: my professor of Canadian literature. I think I fell in love with him partly because he was the first avowedly Christian person I'd met who took literature seriously as a way to express and understand the issues of creation. Our friendship lasted six excellent years. Through his tutelage and friendship I realized that God valued my mind, that God wanted me to write what was in me to write -- not to make people "feel good," but to make them reach out, question, and grow.

And I met women, none of them professed Christians, none of them lesbian, who really loved me, whom I loved, through all our changes, growth, and discovery. I had spent so much time trying to be acceptable to men that their steadfast love came almost as a surprise. They were the first people I had known since the death of my grandmother who loved and valued me for the things I loved and valued in myself.

My honored teacher would not be happy to know that our relationship had as one of its fruits my self-acceptance of my lesbianness. Like many otherwise fine Christians, he possessed an ignorant hatred of gayness and his intellect generally rolled over and played dead whenever *any* issue of sexuality was tabled. He gave me much else, though, that I could keep and use, including a deep affection for my chosen Anglican church.

Not everyone in my life was the same. When I said to my heart-friend Arwen, "I'm a lesbian," she cheered, and with good reason. She knew that I had at last come out of the dark closet into the bright sun of full life.

With genuine love and acceptance from most friends, all of my family, some of my teachers and clergy, and of course lovers, I had it easy by the standards of most of the lesbians or gay men whose stories I know. God's love has stalwartly supported me, so much so that, even in my times of greatest darkness, when nothing made sense or had form or purpose, not even my own personhood, I could say to God, "I don't understand this; I'm unhappy, but I know You are with me. Whatever happens, whether I go insane or get well, I know You will never desert me." It was not a plea for reassurance, but a statement of incontrovertible certainty.

I got well. I write more and better, even being published occasionally as a poet and polemicist. I am more confident and effective in my daily life and work. I'm more than ever committed to working for a just and loving world, for a truly inclusive, loving and Christ-following church. My relationships are more than ever based on love and mutual respect and help, whatever their sexual content. I have much more energy now that I'm not fighting and denying myself half my time.

I am ashamed of the ignorance and brutality I see in the church, which is supposed to be unlike secular society, but behaves exactly like it with respect to gays and lesbians. Many who call themselves Christians--some of them clergy--are proud of being ignorant, vicious, and rejecting. They refuse to know much. It sickens me to think of the damage they do to their immortal souls in their contented hatred.

I believe that gayness will someday be understood for what it is: a normal variation in the spectrum of human sexuality, a manifestation of human nature that presents itself uniformly and statistically consistently across history, class and culture. Suppression, despite what the homophobes say, is not a valid way to live. Celibacy is a gift, and rarely given, in my experience and observation (and also, incidentally, in Christ's), and it ought to be that way. I know that God is concerned with ethics and the intent of the heart and not, as Harrison Ford said, with how the plumbing works.

I believe God led me out of the slavery of shame, deceit and fear into a freedom I could not have predicted ten years ago so that I could be a more effective witness and friend to the dispossessor and the dispossessed in God's world. I believe God created me lesbian as the best affectional "fit" for my personality and gifts: God made me gay as God made me a writer, because it was well to do so. I am free to love, free to be who I am, free to be fully responsible--sexually, creatively and humanly--to my God, because I am not ashamed, not self-denying. Many despise, hate and fear me, sometimes without having met me. How can they hear me when I tell them: "I am happy, fulfilled, productive, at peace"? Are these the fruits of sin or illness? The happiness and peace which Christ continuously gives to me, his lesbian follower, most seriously challenge all who would change me or deny my witness.

Richard Kerr's Story

Although we were taught that it is not nice to talk openly of one's sexuality, I share my experience because not
to do so is to make common cause with forces which
threaten completely to undo the Church's mission.
These forces encourage each of us to hide the truth and
thereby deny our Name, "God With us." These forces
build on keeping our truth untold: they encourage hatred, violence and even murder. To rationalize these
dreadful consequences, some Christians narrowly value
the parts of the Bible which call for violence toward
those who are different. My story displays the effects of
hiding the truth, especially the danger to the Church.

I was not openly gay when I was ordained 27 years ago.
I did not hide the truth in order to be ordained. Society
and the Church had succeeded in keeping me from
knowing the truth about myself.

In junior high school my interest in the Church blos-
somed in response to the friendships shared with various Christians. I found in the Church loving people
and a place where loving relationships seemed to be
the norm. The Church was wonderfully different from
football, whose only goal, to my mind, was to teach us
how to endure pain or to inflict pain upon others for
me amusement of onlookers. Certainly, that form of
athletic activity provided me no pleasure. The Church
was vividly and grandly different.

At the same time I was finding out that what I wanted
to do in secret with other boys was not only
"nasty"--adult words for it---but also "dangerous." Such
boys were often beat up by the boys who didn't "do it"
with each other. "Normal" boys slandered the other

boys. For a Suburban boy of the 50's, being gay was profoundly traumatic. The Church referred to this issue only obliquely, always to advise, "Don't do it," because God hates it. This teaching confused me utterly, but the Church brooked no questions.

The schools added to my confusion. My class was the first in Denver to have formal sex education classes. These meetings over the years constituted a powerful support to all the other forces which urged us not to know ourselves. We were told repeatedly that the only way any decent person behaved was to date people of the opposite sex. It really is an error to say "we" were told, because "we" implies some community being addressed. In fact, most of us who were gay in 1950's suburbia were so traumatized by homophobia both overt and covert, that we were unable to talk with each other of our feelings and experiences. From age five through college, despite having sexual contacts with three other males, I never had a conversation about that experience with any of my partners. I reached thirty-eight before I was able to speak of my own feelings and experiences to other gays who would speak openly of their own experiences. Such radical silence is known historically in only the most repressive and tyrannical regimes, usually named today "Stalinist," a more than apt word to describe the atmosphere in which gays grew up in the 50's.

In high school, I was induced to date girls both as a religious duty and, I thought, as a way to survive the episodic beatings of gays about which we heard. Despite my discomfort, I found one girl whose company was more pleasant than any others. We dated steadily. During my second year in high school we decided to marry nine years later, after I had completed all my education and ordination to the priesthood. For the rest of high school I succeeded at not expressing my attraction to boys, at least so far as anyone on the outside could tell. Inwardly, there was no change whatsoever.

In college I read everything I could find in the library about homosexuality, without any awareness whatsoever that the library of a major Church liberal arts college had a pitifully small number of volumes about the subject, none of which in any way whatever gave anything like an honest portrayal of the subject. The teaching of the Church and all other "experts" seemed to me to be that homosexuality was a way station on the journey from childhood to adulthood. Adults who failed the transformation to heterosexuality always were cursed by God and became child molesters. The picture was so horrific that it convinced me beyond reasonable doubt that I was not homosexual. The Church gave no permission for me to explore my feelings honestly with anyone, nor to link my behavior with those feelings. Even a hint that a person was homosexual brought, in my community, severe social condemnation.

When, consequently, I had a single homosexual contact as a college junior, I was so traumatized by my enjoyment of the experience that I was married within six weeks. I knew that the time had come for my transformation into a proper heterosexual --- that I could no longer postpone my sexuality. At age twenty, then, I had embarked on the Church's only course toward holy sexuality; yet my involuntary feelings remained entirely unchanged. Although I was successful at sexual intercourse with my wife, my fantasies which accompanied our lovemaking were always of other men.

When I came into the formal ordination process, I was terrified that the homosexual kernel of my being would

155

be discovered during my psychological examination, but I did not lie when asked any question about myself, and I was duly certified for ordination from a psychological perspective. No one asked if I were homosexual during any part of the process. I was ordained in 1963. I served parishes in Montana and suburban Colorado in the early part of my ministry, continuously pressed by my feelings toward men, but never acting on them.

Finally, while serving a as rector in Denver, and as Secretary of the Executive Council of the Diocese, I could no longer internalize the contradictions which society and the church had laid upon me. I divorced my wife, even then not able to say even to myself that the divorce happened because I was gay, although my wife knew it to be "the problem." Soon, however, I knew that I was gay. That occurred while I served on a task force on human sexuality for the diocese of Colorado. I had begged the bishop to appoint one or more openly gay persons to that task force, but he refused. And so I brought to the deliberations of that group only my closeted, deeply confused and terrified sexuality.

There was never any intent that meaningful discussion about the issue occur in Colorado. General Convention has mandated the Church to study sexuality, but the penalty for honesty among clergy -- loss of employment -- entirely prevents the Church from developing anything approximating the truth. In Colorado our study group in the mid-70's had one or two straight people who had a measure of sympathy and human understanding, but it was dominated by people whose primary qualification was their rampant ignorance of who gay and lesbian people are, and their unqualified unwillingness to learn from them or from anyone the facts which would enable even the beginning of informed judgment as to the nature, let alone the ethics, of homosexuality.

Of much more meaning were the discussions I had with a gay priest and his lover, both of whom the Church had treated abysmally because they were known to be gay. After meeting these men, I saw my closet as a coward's paradise. I knew without doubt that if I were to "come out" that I would become unemployable in the Church. However, I could not stomach employment built on dishonesty.

My parish was in a very poor section of Denver, and its members were primarily African Americans. I ignorantly concluded that the gay issue concerned primarily middle or upper class whites. I felt that to acknowledge my sexual identity publicly would inflict upon a group already taxed by prejudice and poverty an alien issue, an issue of an advantaged group of whites. I was assisted in this decision by a young black associate, who manifested the homophobia ubiquitous in our society. He insisted that the black community had crucial objectives, which did not include homosexuality, and, in my isolation and confusion I accepted his judgment.

During my almost ten years as rector, the buildings of the church literally fell down around us, and we undertook an enormous building project. I had led the effort which raised half a million dollars, supervised the construction project, and developed a dynamic parish life. I had also been one of the principal leaders in the project to desegregate the Denver Public School System. I was, plainly, exhausted. I am certain that this exhaustion contributed to my decision to resign before coming out. I also believe, however, that I already had been infected with the AIDS virus, and the weakness caused by the virus contributed to my inability to see the truth: that homosexuality knows no racial, ethnic or national boundaries. It is a universal phenomenon, a simple fact-from-the-womb of all human societies, not an index to moral depravity.

I resigned in mid-1979, a few months before the Denver General Convention. My decision let the Church in Colorado off the hook; my "coming out" would not help it discover a deeper truth about human sexuality. I later learned that just at this time, The Reverend William Barcus, an associate in a San Francisco Parish had come out during a sermon. He seemed to me a heroic figure, because of his willingness to bear social hatred so that the Church might learn the truth.

During the 1979 General Convention, Presiding Bishop John Allin agreed to dedicate the entirely renewed parish buildings. I was invited to concelebrate the dedicatory mass with him, and to say a few words. Perhaps because the President of the House of Deputies was an African American, he chose with his friends to attend that Sunday service, and about thirty bishops of the church were present. In all about 600 people heard me recall that we had named the new structure "All Saints Community Wing" of Holy Redeemer Church because the structure had been built with the contributions of many, many hundreds of people to assist the realization of the aspirations of many who needed the Church's support because of poverty or social rejection. I then listed the many various groups which had need of the shelter the Community Wing could provide and the support the Church devoted and pledged itself to give. I concluded my remarks saying "and the gay community, of which I am a part, needs your loving support and help."

To my astonishment everyone broke into applause, and I felt each of the 600 people present tried to touch me during the kiss of peace, offering love and support. Though my "coming out" was low key and not intrusive into the day's celebration, it was clearly understood by those present at the service, which included an ordinary Christian community, and the leadership of the national Church.

Yet, within a week the bishop of the diocese called me to his office. He accused me of being a liar and worse for not revealing clearly to him that I was gay and committed himself to insure that I would never again serve in the Church. His opposition to gay people was legendary already in the Church, and his mistreatment of clergy known to be gay should be in any history ultimately written about gay people in the Church. Should I have chosen to come out to him, I could justifiably have been marked psychologically as being suicidal. So, as previously noted, I had resigned the parish and had a job outside his control by the time these events transpired.

Despite the fact that I have wanted to continue a ministry to which I was called when I was 16 years old, my relationship with the Church as a priest whose ministry is supported by the Church essentially ended at this time. Although I am still a priest in good standing and on cordial terms with my bishop, I have never been able to secure a job as a priest since coming out. Were such a job offered me at this point, it is doubtful I could do it because AIDS has so drained me of strength.

Life has taught me that regret is worthless. Instead, it is now time to face the Church with the consequences of its failure truly to understand human sexuality, and, particularly, to honor homosexual persons, who, though a statistical minority of the Church, contribute much of the energy, vibrant love and intelligent faith which are the keystones of the Church. I believe that the Church can rightly be called to account in my own case. I am literally a child of the Church, an individual whose values and major life experiences took place within the Church and as a result of the received faith of the Church.

Because I have paid attention to the Church's teachings about homosexuality, I believe that I deeply injured a woman whom I married in good faith by being unable to fulfill the marriage vows of the Church. I believe the divorce which became necessary for me if I were not entirely to lose my sanity created a grief which is still virtually a daily experience for me, for my wife, for each of our children and for both our families. I believe that the Church's failure to listen to its gay people, and to encourage them to share their experience openly and honestly has deprived the Church of a vast body of extremely talented priests. The diocese of California alone has hundreds of men who are not employed as priests primarily because they are gay and living in the San Francisco community which is one of the more hospitable communities for gay and lesbian people in the United States. And yet, even in this most positive of communities, many priests still hide their sexuality out of fear for their jobs.

The Church is not well-served by a reactionary rejection of homosexual persons. Those who are in Church closets lead lives of quiet desperation. Their best gifts are perverted by the energy they have to exert hiding. And, particularly the children of the church who happen to be lesbian or gay are terribly injured by the fact that there are too few role models for them --- individuals who openly and faithfully serve the Church and who are obviously lesbian or gay. There is utterly no excuse for the demand made by most congregations that their priest be a married person in order to be a proper role model for the children. Such an assumption is based on the erroneous belief that all the children are strictly heterosexual, or that it is better to be heterosexual, and, therefore, every effort must be made to ensure that they are influenced in that direction. In fact homosexuality is natural throughout all living things, though statistically it is not as common as heterosexuality.

Living the lie, the Church deprives itself of creative energies, which it can ill afford to lose. The great loss in numbers of members is as easily attributable to the Church's hatred of lesbian and gay people, African Americans, and women, as it is to the halting steps taken in the last decades to involve these minorities in the life of the Church.

It is far past time, I believe, for those of us who are lesbian and gay, to demand that the Church, whether on the national or the local level, honor our devoted service. We must insist that the Prince of Peace and the Lord of Love is the true Symbol of the Church. The battle over acceptance of lesbian and gay people really is a battle about the fundamental nature of God. Do we worship the Living God who has created us gay and straight, black and white, male and female; or do we worship an icon of prejudice? Is the Messiah the Lord of Love, or is he the one who throws the first stone at one who is different? Is Christianity a religion of Truth, or is it a weekly Klan meeting?

Second David's Story: A Letter from Prison

I have been active in gay Christian circles since 1978, traveling thousands of miles each year, just to be with one or two gay men having trouble coming to terms with their sexuality, the community, and the Church. Rural isolation exacerbates "coming out." Idaho, Montana, Wyoming, Washington, Oregon, and Utah was "our territory." We spent most of our time in Idaho, Montana, Wyoming, and Eastern Washington though. For the past ten years we put on the average of 20,000 miles a year traveling for our ministry. It was truly the spirit of God at work, the way things happened.

Joe and I were always active in the Church (as Mike and I had been too). I was liturgically and musically active; Joe was an organizer, a great cook, and Mr. "Fix It."

It was surprising that when Joe died and our relationship became front page news and barroom gossip, so many people acted astonished at the revelation. The same people that had sent only one Christmas card addressed "To David and Joe," only one dinner party invitation addressed "To David and Joe," only one wedding invitation, one graduation announcement.... the same people that would ask me "Where's Joe?" or "How's Joe?" if I would show up at a gathering alone, the same people that would ask Joe "Where's David?" or "How's David?" if Joe showed up alone. The same people that saw Joe, me, and the children in church, shopping, working, and playing together.

I had never before experienced any hypocrisy or rejection. Only the great outpouring of love from most in the Church and from our friends offset the pain of grief and rejection by a few.

In 1976 we went to a weekend retreat in the Diocese of Montana in Missoula. We met two other men that "shared a house." They invited us to stay over. After one day together we had no secrets. Joe and I had matching wedding bands--which to an observant person said it all. After sharing with Richard and Kevin for the next year, they too decided to make their commitment before God and witnesses. Joe and I stood with them as their "best men." Through Kevin and Richard, Joe and I were gradually introduced to several other gay men in Missoula when we visited, and we met others on our own. At a small dinner party one evening, I said it was a shame that many of us didn't gather together as a "family" more often. I truly believe the Spirit was directing me that night. Before the evening was over we had set the wheels in motion for an organization we had named "Out in Montana."

It snowballed. Within a year, we had a monthly news-letter with a mailing list of 500! We had monthly dances with statewide draw, which quickly became weekly. It was beautiful to see people from the same little rural community "meet each other" at these affairs. The surprised expressions--"John, I never would have guessed!" "Tom, what are *you* doing here!?" "Jim, I always wondered about you, but was afraid to ask." The warmth and camaraderie that grew from these events was almost electric. Our Memorial Day and Labor Day affairs were soon four-day events. Halloween and New Year's always held additional exciting events. Most important of all, people returned home feeling better about themselves, with new friendships often from their own hometown.

In our second year we established the Hot Line telephone which helped many others come out. Especially the cowboy/loggers/miners and other macho types.

The original "founding fathers" still met for dinner and discussion at least once a month. I usually was asked to say grace before the meal and began offering prayers for those in need. I even delivered an occasional homily when needed, and then I added a prayer asking God to bless our going out into the world to do the work.

The month after I started asking a blessing at our regular meeting, it was decided that we should meet on a regular basis for a service/discussion/study. We included an invitation in our next news to all interested people. Thirty people attended our first Gay Christian Support Group meeting. I read Morning Prayer and we began our discussions. What was intended only as a Saturday morning meeting lasted all day with dinner and socializing in the evening. We went dancing as a group that evening and by example did some evangelizing, inviting all to learn about Jesus Christ and the peace he offers. I remember well a comment I overheard that night: "Boy, those Christians sure know how to love, and they can have fun too."

For our second meeting, people arrived from all over Montana. One newcomer I recognized as a close associate of the Bishop. We talked about how the Bishop might react to open discussion. I decided that I needed to have the Bishop's approval in the form of a lay-reader's license. I already had one, plus a license to preach in the Diocese of Spokane. Somewhat apprehensive, I went to explain to the Bishop my ministry to gay people of Montana, Idaho, Wyoming and Washington. He was supportive and issued me a license on the spot, and he suggested some parishes where we might inquire about meeting space. He said he would discreetly mention our group to some folk when the opportunity arose. Within six months, Joe and I had helped start six other groups around the state.

The Gay Christian Support Group Network was on the move, and so was my active ministry to the gay community. Joe and I often drove all night, taking turns sleeping and driving, to get from place to place in time for a gathering or appointment.

Word of our groups soon spread. We often had visitors from out of state. The Rev. Sylvia Pennington, author of *But Lord, They're Gay* and *Good News for Modern Gays* became a close personal friend of ours. Joe often referred to her as his adopted mother. Morris Floyd, a national figure for gay recognition in the Methodist Church, also visited frequently. Jerry Browning, composer/performer of gay Christian music, was one of the early members and a party in the first Gay Union held after our group formed. Sylvia officiated.

In 1980, after much prayer, Joe and I decided we needed more time to spend on our ministry, so we retired from our Law Enforcement Careers, and became seasonal employees of the U. S. National Park Service. We worked 4-6 months a year and then had the remainder to devote full-time to our ministry. It required a major re-adjustment financially, but it was much easier than anticipated. Having the house and cars paid for and no payments to speak of to make was a big help. With the youngest child 11 and the oldest 18, we didn't feel too guilty about extended trips leaving a housekeeper in charge. Our reputation seemed to grow overnight. Calls came in regularly from the four-state area seeking advice, a visit, affirmation, love. We put together an all-day program which we named "a Kiss Me Day." It was designed to bring people in touch with themselves and others around them to help them over the tough times. It was successful. In the fall of 1980 we started building the foundation for a support group serving North Idaho. In the Spring of 1981, the North Idaho Network (NIN) became a reality. It too enjoyed bounding success. Our Gay Christian Support Group in North Idaho acted in conjunction with one we helped establish in Spokane to form the core group that became Emmanuel MCC in Spokane. Our group in Billings, Montana, became Family of God MCC. In the other large cities, Missoula, Great Falls, Helena, Bozeman, Kalispell, and Havre, the groups either filtered people back to their "home churches" or they found a new home at a "friendly church." The major groups continued to exist for study and discussion. At last count, most of the smaller groups in rural communities were still vital. The Spirit definitely decided what was to happen to each group. In 1983, we began work in Yellowstone National Park; we had spent earlier seasons in Glacier National Park. This was the time when our Wyoming ministry began to flourish. Grand Teton National Park is just south of Yellowstone. There you will find the Chapel of the Transfiguration, circa 1925. It was a mission of St. John's in Jackson, Wyoming--a vital, exciting, warm parish. During the summer they employed a full-time chaplain, a retired priest. Our first year in Yellowstone, I was licensed by the Bishop of Wyoming as Lay Minister and Chalice Bearer. I assisted at the Wednesday Eucharist every week at St. John's, Jackson, at noon and at the Chapel at 4 p.m. Because of illness, as I recall, the chaplain had to leave late in August. I continued Wednesday services as Evening Prayer. To my surprise, one Wednesday shortly before service was to begin, I was joined by the Bishop of Wyoming. He had his own plane and was famous for "dropping in." After the service we had a long talk which included dinner into the evening. I had introduced Joe as my life-mate and his only comment on that was, "How long have you two been together?" I replied nearly 10 years, and he said, "sounds permanent to me" and that was that. We talked mostly about the mission of the Church, evangelism and my outreach ministry to the gay community. I made some recommendations to him about services in and about Yellowstone. During the winter, I put my ideas into writing. During the Spring Lay Readers Conference, he pulled me aside and said, "I like your ideas; make definite plans; let me know what I can do to help. I'll send you a revised license. Oh, where is Joe?" I told him Joe was with friends and would join us at dinner. "Good, good," he said. "I'll look forward to seeing him." I later learned that was the closest the Bishop ever came to giving us his approval. That summer I began having three services a week in Yellowstone, with scheduled visits monthly from neighboring priests for Eucharist. That is another interesting story, with some pain.

During our last season in Yellowstone, before Joe's death, Sylvia Pennington planned to use our home as her base for reaching out to Wyoming. Sudden illness prevented this. We had invited nearly 100 people to join us for a 4th of July "Camp Out" to meet Sylvia. Sixty showed up and we had a terrific sharing in the outdoors.

I did consider ordination, at the encouragement of my three bishops. I was just completing my first year in the

Diocesan School of Theology when my world fell apart. It is a three-year program designed to prepare one for ordination as a permanent deacon. No promises or guarantees were made. Either way the education would be well received.

Now that I am in prison I feel so lonely, as if on an island in a sea of negativity. Without my faith, I would have been lost long ago. You see, I was the Chief of Police of a city in Northern Idaho at one time. That makes me hated by all inmates. The few Christian inmates that could overlook that "defect in my character" cannot overlook the fact that I am gay! The fundamentalists control all religious functions here, and you know where that leaves me. My reputation, "gay activist," preceded me thanks to the gay bashing the press gave me. They are afraid I will organize some type of outreach to other gay people inside, and they have all but forbidden me to do this. An Episcopal priest does come in once a month, and I am permitted to assist him with the Eucharist. I have no one inside that I can even begin to talk to, let alone relate to, and this pains me. I have been raised as a servant of Christ from the cradle, by a warm, loving, caring Irish family. My grandparents emigrated. Being forbidden to function in this manner is doubly oppressive to me.

I was 16 before I knew there was any social life outside the Church. Mom was organist, Dad a deacon. I was in the choir until my voice changed, then served as an acolyte and youth leader. I served on the Bishop's Youth Advisory Council, in the province, and for the Presiding Bishop also. I "denied" the call to ministry when my school counselors convinced me my country needed my engineering skills, in 1958. At 8, I was shown why I had "different feelings" by a neighbor boy, 14. At 16 my best friend and I made a commitment to each other before God to be life-mates. We were together for fifteen years, through college, the Air Force, and the building of a business.

After 10 years of being together, Michael and I decided that the only thing missing from our "marriage" was children. We both had much love we wanted to bestow on a child. We tried foster parenting, but that was temporary and parting was painful. Open adoption in "redneck country" was out of the question; private adoption costs were almost unrealistic, and we had other reservations about it also. Instead, we selected a willing young woman to be the mother of our children. To circumvent legal and insurance problems, I married her. We set her up with a job and a home (our summer home). Jennifer was born in 1967 and Eric in 1968. We told everybody that we acquired the children by private adoption. We quietly terminated the arrangement with Kathy. The children both use our combined last names.

Those were definitely growing times for us all. Our patterns changed drastically. Michael stayed home and took on the role of primary care-giver. After 6 months, I rearranged my work profile so that I worked at home three days a week, and at the office two. We hired a housekeeper, and Michael returned to work on the same schedule as I. One of us was almost always at home, to be a bonding parent. It was a wonderful time in our lives. Many of our friends thought we were crazy. Actually we were -- crazy in love with each other and our children. They were our children, since Michael and I were the same blood type. Because of the manner in which conception took place, it was impossible to determine whose sperm had "done the job."

A year after Eric was born, the biological mother married a real jerk. When he found out what she had done for us, he tried to blackmail us. That was when we found out what a wonderful job our lawyer had done for us when the temporary marriage was terminated. Included in the papers was a document entitled "termination of parent-child relationship" which Kathy had willingly signed. That took the wind out of his sails, especially when our attorney threatened criminal charges against him.

That was the only "bad scene" we had involving our children.

While Michael was returning home from a business trip in our plane, a sudden snow storm caused his death on a mountain top. His death left me a "widower" with two children.

When Jennifer and Eric were 6 and 5 respectively, I explained briefly their origin. A year later I took them to meet their biological mother, who I had just learned was dying of cancer. Michael and I had planned on doing this together at an appropriate time. I felt that this was important, as Joe's children were still talking about their mother. Michael's fatal plane crash had occurred two years earlier, so the decision rested on my shoulders. I hope I did the right thing.

More recently I discussed this with Jennifer and Eric. Each remembers Michael as one would remember a deceased mother. They are both normal young adults.

About a year after Michael's death, a business associate came to see me. His wife had run off and left him with three children. Financially and spiritually he was drowning. I got him involved in the Church and did what I could to keep him from financial ruin. We became close friends, hunting, fishing, camping and socializing together. Mike and I had built a nice big home. It soon became obvious that Joe was going to lose his. I offered to let him share my home. With the children we came up short a bedroom. Until we could add one, we shared a bedroom. There was no indication up till then that he was gay. Soon afterwards, Joe told me that he was gay, and we began our 14-year relationship.

Joe's family were all alcoholics, as Joe himself had become, during his teens. Shortly after I met him, he had given up drinking but understood that he was a "recovering" alcoholic. In the fall of 1986, he associated at work with a crowd of heavy drinkers and drank more than he could handle. Twice between October and December he had voluntarily gone through detoxification, the second time under a doctor's care. This recovery was coming along nicely. We planned an extended trip beginning the middle of January. At 6 a.m. on January 3, 1987, my birthday, he awoke me with a pistol in my face. He said, "I am going to shoot you." I tried to get the gun away from him, and it went off. Joe died and my world collapsed.

The coroner's report showed that he had taken a whole month's supply of anti-depressant, and had drunk a fifth of vodka. The pathologist's report hinted at a cerebral hemorrhage, but because of the bullet's damage, it was inconclusive. The local newspaper was vicious. It hinted at a lovers' quarrel, describing us as both clad only in t-shirts when the police arrived. They were actually thermal knit knee length night shirts. The "faggots" became the talk of the town. The religious and gay community rallied to my support, but the political pressure by the "red necks" resulted in my arrest for second-degree murder. The religious community poured out love, the greatest gift I have ever received. With the Dean's consent and the Bishop's approval, we held a memorial service for Joe at the Cathedral of St. John in Spokane. Our blessed union was recognized, and I was acknowledged as the surviving spouse, a first for the Diocese. It was a fitting memorial to Joe as from that time on, Integrity's position in the Diocese has grown positively. Last fall, Integrity was invited to have a booth at Diocesan Convention, which, given our Bishop, we feel to be one step short of "official" recognition.

The sordid part of the story is that I have been ruined financially. An unscrupulous attorney has convinced Joe's parents to sue me for everything. They may even be able to take the trust fund set up for our children. I wonder if my pain will ever cease?

Joe's children have gone their separate ways and since the trial have come under the influence of Joe's father, who is trying to persuade them that I'm a sick, vicious individual responsible for their father's death. I know that the children know better. It has been a month since I've heard from any of them.

Jennifer has moved here to Boise to be close to me. I see her and her husband Myron weekly and usually call her midweek. I talk to Eric at least once a week. He is coming to Boise later this month for a couple of weeks before entering the Marines.

I'm sure there are those that would take exception to what Michael and I did to "have" Jennifer and Eric, but they have never known a moment without love. They were never without a parent that had time to listen. There is nothing I would do different save not having bought the plane Michael died in.

I know God is working in my life. I must believe that. I can acknowledge that perhaps I had too much, but I had committed it all to outreach to the gay community. We had an attorney working on setting up a foundation to educate and counsel gay youth. We had committed property to establish a "halfway" house for troubled gay youth. This has all been lost because of my incarceration. I can believe God may want to take my riches from me, but I still can't understand why Joe was taken from me or the work we started for gay youth.

For "killing" Joe, the judge sentenced me to 20 years indeterminate, which means that I will be considered for parole in five years. I do have an appeal pending for a new trial. The State Supreme Court may hear it in a few months.

It is time for lights out. Agape.

Steve's Story

Dear Mom and Dad,

The postscript on your last letter has prompted this fast reply, though I have long considered how I should write this letter and how you would receive it.

I am a homosexual. I am not sick, nor deviate, nor mentally ill. My sexuality simply expresses itself in attraction for other men rather than women. Neither is it unnatural. I am not attracted to children nor pain nor heterosexual men. For me it is completely natural and right and good.

If your morality would condemn me, first consider these things: I did not choose to be homosexual, but I found myself one and have accepted it, happily as an integral part of my personality; the morality that would condemn me for something over which I had no control must itself be without humaneness, akin to the consciousness which gassed Jews and massacred Indians. Homosexuals in this and other countries have for centuries been forced to lead secretive lives, in constant fear that their careers would be destroyed and their relationships with loved ones cut off.

I refuse to hate myself and I refuse to allow anyone who wishes to have continued personal contact with me to hate this essential part of my self either. I also refuse to live in the half world of gay ghettos, where fugitive sexual liaisons pass for love and self-revulsion and secretiveness are the prevailing mode.

I do not live a life surrounded only by gay men. All my friends, both in Idaho and here have, for a long time, accepted this facet of my personality without reservation, knowing that I was a whole being, not divisible into acceptable or unacceptable parts. My two beautiful sisters have shown me only warmth and love and remarkable understanding, as I hope my brother will when he is old enough to comprehend the implications of the oppressive social stigma attached to my sexuality.

I will not live a life of fear and shame. Too many important matters interest me for me to spend my life concerned with other peoples' unjust and inhumane moral prejudices. I only hope that I can find one person, one man, with whom I might share the rest of my life as you two have shared yours. And though I will not have children, I hope to involve myself in my nieces and nephews and share the pleasure of their growing.

It is very important that you, as parents, not feel guilty because I, your son, am a homosexual. Guilt implies fault and fault implies a misdeed, and I cannot consider myself as some mistake to be altered if at all possible, someone to be accepted only with resignation. I must ask you to accept me fully, as a human being worthy of respect and trust and love. I am not less than any other being simply because I am a homosexual!

Obviously, I am involved in the Gay Liberation Movement. I wish that you would look for these books and read them, so that you might have a better understanding of gay problems and aspirations: *Homosexual Oppression and Liberation; Society and the Healthy Homosexual; The Gay Mystique*; and *The Gay Militants*.

Finally, I hope that you can accept this part of me without reservations and regrets. You may fault Dr. Stromberg as a failure, but before his therapy I had despised myself, and he helped me gain a measure of self-respect, which was a great service. I believe that your capacity to love can encompass the totality of my self and that you will know that I am the very same son that you have known for 21 years. If I disappoint you, I am sorry, but I cannot spend my life in apology. I must look to the future and so must you. I would appreciate a rapid reply to this letter.

All my love, your son, Steve.

-- October 13, 1972

Allen's Story

The following encounter led me to reflect on the implications of my faith as a gay male during these times. I am 34 and was confirmed in the Episcopal Church ten years ago.

Each Monday night I serve as an AIDS Hotline volunteer in a major city. One night I received a call from a distraught young man I'll call Tony. Tony was depressed, nauseated, and unable to eat -- for good reason. He had just been informed that he tested positive for infection by HIV -- human immunodeficiency virus.

Over the course of a 45-minute conversation we touched on many topics, including research, health, support mechanisms, faith, and our roles in this crisis. I said that Tony had an important role to play as a sero-positive (infected) individual; namely, to work at maintaining his level of physical, psychological, and spiritual well-being while trusting the diligence and expertise of others as they work on more efficacious treatments for the disease. Providentially, clinics now help those infected monitor their health and avoid re-infection and groups support them and share their concerns. But how can we preserve spiritual equilibrium in these times? Where is God in all this?

According to the biblical witness, God sides with the afflicted and oppressed, God actively liberates and restores. One has only to witness the quantity and variety of responses to AIDS from care-givers, counselors, AIDS funding lobbyists, volunteers, and researchers to acknowledge that the Holy Spirit still beckons us to work for healing and reconciliation.

Tony is black; I am white. We never met and will probably never even speak again on the telephone. Yet by the end of our conversation we both perceived something of the interrelatedness of human life. In our efforts to end this scourge we share in one another's lives and ultimately the larger life of the universe and God. Personally, I find spiritual sustenance through worship in my parish and Integrity services. In particular, I find my rector's insistence on spiritual development and the ministry of the laity helpful.

At the conclusion of the call, Tony reported his appetite had returned. I continue to pray for him and all others affected by HIV, with the hope that working in concert we may alleviate some of the pain and suffering caused by AIDS and in the process rediscover God in our midst.

Second Ralph's Story

I grew up in Ohio in a Catholic family. At 32 I became an Episcopalian, in 1959.

When I was growing up, my family almost forced me to go to church. I enjoyed being an altar boy and singing in the choir, but everything else was by rote! I was the youngest of six, with ten years between my sister and me.

When I was born, only my sister was home, so I learned to cook, clean and sew, while my brothers all went hunting and fishing.

Sports never interested me. I enjoyed dancing with the girls until they tried to seduce me. I was petrified.

I suspected I was gay in high school, but I can't remember any experiences.

I went into the military service and the week before I was to get out, some kissing went on.

Back home, I worked in a decorating studio. One day the buyer drove me home, took me to dinner, and said, "It's all up to you." I did not know what he meant. He told me not to fall in love with him as he was going to get married.

I wound up in sales for 21 years and did very well, so that after 10 years I had a house. I wanted to share my success with someone. I could not face society living with a man. My wife and I had one wonderful son. I had discreet affairs while on the road. After my wife died of cancer, I decided I would come out of the closet and wrote many friends that I was going to Spain with a gay professor. My only concern was my son. He came home and caught me kissing someone in the kitchen one night. That solved how I should tell him! He has taken it very well, and we are closer now than ever.

I have been on the vestry, in the choir, and on the flower committee. I think half of the parish knows I am gay, but others I am not sure of. I was upset when our "open-minded" priest would not allow two lesbians to come up to the rail together to celebrate their anniversary! I wrestled with the fact that if I didn't accept myself, then I did not like God, who made me. It took years for God to convince me that he likes me and wants me to like myself so that I can love others. To this day, I have never really been in love with anyone and am not convinced that I can love anyone.

I was taught "All sex is bad." To this day I have trouble with erections, but I refuse to spend thousands of dollars on the couch!

I was delighted to join Integrity but am upset that we cannot meet in the Cathedral, reportedly because they fear we are fostering evil doings, women's rights, and other "bizarre things." Things also went negatively at our Diocesan Convention.

On my job for all my life I have lived in fear that someone might find out that I am gay. Since I have only four months left before I retire from my job at the V.A., I have decided to come out to fight for the right to be accepted as what I am, a gay Christian.

I hope that younger people will not have to go through the same fears all their lives.

William's Story

As a little boy, I was a devout Southern Baptist. I said my prayers each and every night without fail, giving thanks to God for family, friends, and neighbors. I took it all very, very seriously. As a teen, all that changed and, for several reasons, I came to target the church for criticism.

It was the early 1970's. Many neighborhoods on the south side of Atlanta had become what were called "transitional neighborhoods." This suburban euphemism meant the racial composition of the neighborhood was changing from completely white to completely black. Our neighborhood, College Park, was one. Our life, even at Headlands Baptist Church, was pervaded by a racial hypocrisy that shaped our conversations and warped our behavior. Racism was strong. I remember my parents' reaction to a young bi-racial couple we saw on the streets of Manhattan during a vacation when I was fourteen. I watched them grimace in disapproval. Being young and naive, I said something along the lines of "maybe they're just good friends." My parents grimaced again. The message was clear, even without words. Even so, my parents, our neighbors, and the people at church steadfastly refused to acknowledge that they might be bigoted. Rather, they claimed they were moving because they were concerned about property values, the quality of education in our schools, etc. There was never any doubt that we would move. So, images of hypocrisy came to dominate my early impression of Christianity, an impression that would stay with me for many, many years.

I began to see the church as a great charade. Our church was a very insulated, dogmatic, conformist group of people who seemed to exist solely to stroke each other in their profession of faith. They did not tolerate doubt. Accepting Christ provided theological insurance. If you "accepted Jesus as your personal Lord and Savior" everything in your life would suddenly take a turn for the better. Bad things happened to evil people only. I was taught that we tithed because the money and blessings would be returned to us several-fold. Even then I felt cheated out of the rich experience of looking at life honestly. Clearly, life was not always what the fundamentalist said it was. We experience sweetness and light, but we also experience darkness and doubt. Faith is our goal, but often doubt is our reality. I was angry. By my early teens, I gave up on the church; and, by my late teens, on my faith. The church had nothing to hold me.

At the same time I was becoming aware of my sexuality. By the time I was thirteen, I knew in a kind of vague way that I was more attracted physically to boys than girls. I was not ashamed of these feelings but did put them at the back of my mind because I felt they weren't appropriate. I didn't consider them a secret but rather a puzzle. I knew I couldn't be homosexual. Of course I never actually knew or even saw someone who was homosexual (or so I thought) but I had learned that homosexuals were sick, pitiful people. Whatever I was, I was neither sick nor pitiful. Looking back I suppose I thought my feelings and fantasies about my male schoolmates were just a fluke and felt that I alone had these feelings.

Even in my late teen years, when I was acutely aware of being attracted to male friends my age, I still did not worry about the feelings themselves. I knew I was different but I still refused to condemn myself.

Nevertheless, those feelings did isolate me from other boys my age. They dated girls because they wanted to; I dated because I was expected to. While most of my classmates were 'going steady' and starting to think about the future relationships and a family, my dating life was just a sham. I was beginning to feel alienated, lonely, and out of place. I had no sense of belonging and went through private periods of loneliness and depression.

When I was nineteen, Michael, a friend on leave from the Air Force, called me up. We had known each other through grade school and had been very close at one point. We went out to dinner and afterwards to a place called Stephen's Saloon. I took one look around the place and saw that it was jammed with young, college-age guys. I couldn't believe it. All these young men, so unstereotypical, so attractive, and so seemingly agreeable, were gay. That experience left me disoriented for several days. On one hand, I felt cheated. I had been cheated out of the knowledge that I could be a happy, healthy gay person and been forced to live in a world that says "no-no-no" to loving, caring for, and sharing with a person of the same sex. At the same time, I felt overjoyed. Here were people who shared my feelings and my history. Maybe there was a place for me in this world after all.

In my college years, I began watching church services on Sunday morning from St. Luke's Episcopal Church in downtown Atlanta. Instead of the sermons that emphasized fear as a motivation for faith, I heard the Rector, Tom Bowers, talk about a type of faith that was totally new to me. He spoke of Jesus as identifying with outcasts. He talked about questioning, about doubt, and about love. Even the liturgy fascinated me. It was beautiful compared to the services I had known as a child, services that consisted of singing a few hymns, listening to a sermon, and then watching an emotional and embarrassing call to "come down the aisle and accept Christ as your Personal Savior." For the second time in a very brief time, I had discovered an "alternate reality," a new and different world that existed alongside the one that was familiar to me. Maybe there was a place for me in the church after all, even with my doubts, even with my sexuality.

I became involved at St. Luke's. I started by attending confirmation class. Later, I joined a study group held weekly by the Rector, sang in the Choir, and served on a lay committee overseeing the work of one of the deacons assigned to our parish. I was openly gay with several of my friends at St. Luke's. Early on in the AIDS crisis, I introduced the Rector to the Executive Director of AID Atlanta, our local AIDS service organization. That meeting led to several AIDS-related support groups meeting weekly at the church.

I am grateful for the Episcopal Church and Integrity. It rescued my faith by assuring me that many other people face the same problems I face. It gave me room to grow without imposing someone else's narrow expectations on me. It acknowledged my doubts without rejecting me. It has given me a religious community where I feel that I belong. For all this, I thank God and I thank the Episcopal Church. I hope we both continue to grow together.

I might participate even more in the life of the church, but I still have a lingering fear of rejection, for I know that even in our church, many people still harbor the same attitudes and stereotypes that have been so much a part of our culture and religious institutions in the past. I'm a realist when it comes to matters political, and I think we'll not see official blessings of relationships among gay people for many years. Yet this realization is, on a deeper level, a very painful one. This year, Daniel and I begin our fourth year together. Our relationship is a caring and committed one, based on fidelity, love, and respect. It began, and it will continue hopefully for the rest of our lives, but likely without official recognition from the church, To deny us a way of consecrating our relationship is to deny the reality of that relationship. For us to accept that sacramental blessing of a relationship is reserved only for a man and a woman would mean accepting the underlying assumptions that our love is not as real, or as noble, or as desirable. We know this to be a lie. This is not just a "cause" for us; it is our lives.

George's Story

Hope brought me to the Episcopal Church. I am new here. Hope that at last I, too, can know the embrace of a church in the worship of our God.

When I read that in his inaugural sermon as Presiding Bishop, Edmund Browning embraced all those who had been hitherto denied the fullest ministry of the church, I thought, "At last a church within which I might return to religion." I welcome a church that sees its role as pastoral rather than condemnatory, supportive and inclusive rather than arrogant, sanctimonious, judgmental, and exclusive.

I have always intuited that I am homosexual. I realized early that I am somehow "different" and that others do not think my difference to be a good thing. By age 14, I confirmed both my predilection and the negative perceptions of it.

I am the eldest son of a Baptist minister. The effects of living in a small community where my family was well-known, where clergy children were expected inherently to be paragons of virtuous conduct to be examples to other children, combined with my having read (covertly) extensively on homosexuality, were to inflict upon me a sense of shame, of a lesser human worth than "normal" people, and isolation from peers and adults alike. Scripture reinforced these feelings of unworthiness and shame inculcated by society, damning me as a perverted human being. Deep scars from childhood remain.

Only in my late twenties did I begin the life-long process of coming out, first to myself, then to family and

186

others important to me. I told my parents when I was 35 years of age. I had intentionally suppressed telling them for 10 years, certain they would reject me. Their reaction was a pro forma statement that I was still their son. They have not mentioned the issue since. That was five years ago.

Telling my family was cathartic. I felt incredibly clean and relieved of a great burden. I had felt it a duty to tell them who I am, and who I always have been, to disclose a significant part of me kept deeply hidden all my life. Their avoidance of the issue since then continues to disappoint and to wound. Most of the friends whom I have told have been amazingly supportive.

I do not know what to expect if I were to come out to my parish. The difficulties the Church has encountered on issues of women clergy, social responsibility for the increasing numbers of hungry and homeless, as well as sexual identity, does not portend a strongly positive response to one acknowledging one's homosexuality. But the fact that the highest levels of the Church openly discuss the issues encourages me.

I hope that our sharing our stories will be as prayerfully received as they are offered. I hope readers will not use our stories to mock or condemn those gay men and lesbians who refuse any longer to remain estranged from the worship of our God by joining the Episcopal Church.

I have paid a high price for being gay, I think. I lost a career. My career as a naval officer was terminated after 12 years of service, six years ago, not for something I had done but only because of who I am. When asked if I was homosexual I replied only with the truth.

While I was discharged honorably, the loss was no less traumatic. The official documentation violates my privacy and denies other opportunities for the rest of my life. The United States Government chooses to make me and others like me outcasts, just as some in organized religion do also. Long years of loyal, dedicated, competent, and caring service come to nothing; they are insufficient to earn the security of a career of one's choosing and advancement on one's demonstrated merit. A circumstance of humanity can and frequently does ruin all one has worked to attain.

Of a dozen recently on a retreat held jointly by the Integrity chapters in Austin and Houston, all but one began in other religious affiliations. While some will perceive the Church's attraction of people like myself as proof that the Episcopal Church is fast becoming a dumping ground for perverts, it should be something about which to rejoice. That is, some of us see the Church as a center of Christian acceptance and love, a witness to the unchurched that God alone is judge.

I did not choose to be gay, just as I did not choose my hair and eye color, or my right-handedness. But I have chosen once again to join the Church, for the Gospel tells me that none of us measure up to the Christian ideal, that we all fall short. Our duty is to live as responsible, wholesome people. God loves us just as we are. When may we expect that the Church of God will embrace us as fellow strivers to live lives of Christian responsibility?

Second Bill's Story

My wife died suddenly when a blood clot struck her in 1965. Married for almost 20 years, we had 2 children.

When my son and daughter went off to college, I took college students into my rather large, comfortable home. By charging them very little, I helped them to complete their education. Four different ones were from India, one from Mexico, one from Puerto Rico, and others from the USA. As far as I know, all were straight. At that time I knew little about gays and lesbians.

In 1971 I returned to the General Theological Seminary for a summer course entitled "Homosexuality, Women's Lib, and Communal Living." It turned out to be one of the best things that ever happened to me, and I came home determined to do all in my power to help lesbians and gays.

Soon the opportunity arose. A local Metropolitan Community Church asked if they could use our chapel Sunday afternoons for their service. They did, for about five or six months, despite protests from some members of the congregation at St. George's. Eventually MCC got their own place.

Two years later, some 38 gay men members were burned to death in a fire in an upstairs bar. The Bishop was indignant when the newspaper reported that the memorial service was held at St. George's. I asked him whether he thought Jesus would have turned them away from His Church. The Bishop asked what I thought he should say when people called his office that day (I heard 100 called!). I replied, "You can say anything you like, Bishop, but I was doing what I thought was the Christian thing."

Gradually I realized my own homosexuality, or, perhaps, bisexuality. I went to gay bars and baths. Soon I fell in love with a young man, nearly 20 years my junior, and after a year or two he moved into my home with me. It was a great relationship, loving and supporting.

Twice I spoke before the City Council here in New Orleans, urging the adoption of an ordinance protecting gays and lesbians. The Roman Catholics and Fundamentalists defeated it each time. Several times I presented resolutions before our Diocesan Convention supporting gays and lesbians. The Bishop refused a vote by ballot, so each time it was defeated.

My lover died in my arms in March 1986, of cancer of the lymph glands. No one from the Church nor the gay community came to the Roman Catholic funeral, though he was the only "family" I had here.

Now, praise God, I have another lover, near my age (80+), and he has brought much joy into my life. We both know that sex is one of God's most wonderful gifts and needs to be enjoyed daily, or at least frequently.

Hopefully, the Church some day will teach that sex--loving and mutual--is okay for everyone, and a real blessing.

Thomas's Story

My rebirth into the Church and my renewed desire for spiritual growth developed during the onset of my relationship with Manuel, an Episcopalian and my partner for four years now. Manuel was the first man I met in the gay community leading both a homosexual life and a religious life. We have been a monogamous couple for four years and share a fulfilling life together.

Twenty-nine years ago I was born into a Roman Catholic family, the third eldest of five children. Baptized as an infant, I received the sacraments of Holy Communion and Confirmation during my elementary and secondary public school years. My family attended Sunday Mass on a somewhat regular basis, except for my father, who believed the Roman Catholic Church to be filled with hypocrisy.

I've blocked out most of the frightening memories of catechism classes during my elementary and secondary public school. Several tyrannical nuns abused me verbally and physically.

Since becoming an Episcopalian four years ago, I have begun to re-learn Christianity. Before I joined the Church of the Transfiguration, I signed up for study classes given by the rector, in order to begin learning about Anglicanism.

Manuel provided me with an opportunity to meet other gay men and lesbians also interested in religion. He brought me to an Integrity service at St. Lukes in the Field one Thursday evening. It was and still is a beautiful experience for me to be with other gay men and lesbians sharing in the Eucharist. The Integrity programs which follow the Thursday evening services have also been extremely beneficial to me by providing me with educational information and spiritual guidance regarding many topics affecting me as a gay Episcopalian. I think Integrity provides a strong positive influence on lesbians and gay men who pursue a religious life.

Since becoming an Episcopalian I have brought my family and friends to Eucharist on several occasions. My parents and some close friends attended my reception at the Church of the Transfiguration. My rebirth into a religious life has brought me, my parents, and my brothers and sisters closer to God.

Father Martin's Story

It is hard to relate my sexuality to my spirituality. I do not think of myself primarily in sexual terms. Spirituality, like hair color, has always been integral to me.

I have always known that I am gay, at least from the age of three or four. Of course, no child knows what it means to be a sexual person, but I became aware of my own sexual interests.

At about the same time, I learned that being different is not an easy thing in this world. Johnny, who lived next door, wore thick glasses and had crossed eyes. He was different. All of us "regular guys" teased and tormented Johnny, who cried a lot. I learned not to show that I was different.

One Sunday in Church School we were doing our best to make Johnny's life miserable. Our teacher broke up the little game and lectured us on how God loved each of us just as we are, and that we must try to love each other. I learned that God loved Johnny -- other kids might not, but God loved Johnny-- and me.

So, very early, I learned that being different means you cry a lot, and being a regular guy takes a lot of work.

Learning, or more accurately reading, has served me well over the 40-odd years that have passed since that day. From Dr. Kinsey, I learned that I was not too different. From college humanities, I learned that a host of gay men and women have made great contributions to our culture and history. From B., R., and C. I learned that other gay men were seeking ordination -- I was not alone. From a kind and supportive priest, I learned that I could say, "I'm gay," and the world would not come to an end or even fall apart. From my course in ethics, I came to understand the difficulties of strict natural law. I learned that relationship and responsibility go hand-in-hand.

I regret that when J. told me during a civil rights march about the hell of trying to pass as a regular white guy, I did not risk letting him know that I understood something of the hell of trying to pass as a regular guy who is white.

I rejoice that I could tell my mother that I am gay.

I regret that I allowed a former girlfriend to believe there was more to our relationship than there could be.

I rejoice that I received a letter from a former parishioner apologizing for calling me a damned faggot twelve years before, and that I can forgive him in Christ.

I regret the fear that welled up in me when a lady started a conversation with me by saying, "Father, I know you are gay." I rejoice when she went on to tell me that she was a lesbian, and that I was the first priest to whom she has been able to reveal herself during the 60 years of her life.

Where am I now? I am gay. I am happy, at least most of the time. Like most Christians I know, my life has been and continues to be filled with regrets and joy -- guilt and grace --sin and forgiveness.

Anne's Story

The Church, our Church, has caused pain for my brothers and sisters. As a representative of the Church, I am ashamed, and as a priest, I feel the pain. I share the pain when I must counsel people who have been refused eucharist because they are gay.

I share the pain when gay Christian couples in committed long-term relationships, including myself, are refused the Church's blessing. I share the pain when people ask how I got through the ordination process and I say I got through because I wasn't out. To get through now at least, you have to lie. I shared the pain this year when a former member of Integrity went back in the closet in order to get ordained and a job--at what personal cost to his own integrity I can only guess.

Something is wrong when the Church says you have to lie to be acceptable as a Christian.

As I have grown in my spiritual journey as a priest, I have come to value integrity and honesty as *the* bottom-line requirements for being in relationship with myself, with others, and with God. At the same time, I am part of a Church who says that lesbians and gay men must be silent to be acceptable in the Church. Gay people are "acceptable" only when they lie.

I am unacceptable in the diocese where I live because I have refused to live entirely in the closet and because I have named the pain as something the Church has caused. I do not have an altar other than Integrity, and I therefore do not have a congregation, other than Integrity, in which to church my children. The pain goes on. I will minister to it in spite of it.

Ara's Story

We humans have many identities: familial, regional, national, ethnic, religious, political, sexual, and the like. I identify myself as a Dostourian, as a resident in the South and in New England, as a citizen of the U.S., as an Armenian, as an Orthodox Christian, as a Marxist socialist, and last but not least, as a gay person. My "coming out" as a gay person has not been easy for me, especially given my religious and ethnic background.

I grew up in New York City in the late Forties and early Fifties in Washington Heights. When I was in my late teens and early twenties, I was active in the church choir. I was already painfully aware of my gay feelings but dared not express them to anyone, believing them an aberration. I thought I was the only person with such feelings. I did bring myself to open up to an Armenian priest (now a bishop) and a deacon (now a priest), both of whom I felt close to and still do. Though both sympathized, they were not helpful since attractions to members of the same sex went beyond their comprehension and experience.

After receiving a B.A. in history and an M.A. in medieval history, I was accepted as a theological student at ETS (now the Episcopal Divinity School) in Cambridge, MA. I had been thinking seriously of entering the priesthood of the Armenian Church for many years, and had been talking to the Primate about the possibility of serving the Church.

In seminary I had my first gay experiences. Up to that time, I had dared not express my sexual feelings. However, my first gay experiences at ETS were not good ones, for I still had deep-seated guilt feelings. At one point I did open up to one of the professors at the school who was my advisor and with whom I felt comfortable. He was quite understanding and seemed to comprehend my dilemma. He helped me get in touch with my feelings and begin to accept myself as a person.

After graduating from seminary, I had intended to do educational work in the Armenian Church. The new Primate told me that it was not possible, since the Church needed me as a parish priest. Therefore, I decided against ordination and took a position as a teacher at Lenox School, a private Episcopal school in Western Massachusetts. I taught there for three years. During those years I still was not completely comfortable with my sexuality, yet I felt that my self-image was improving.

After three years at Lenox, I decided to go into college teaching and entered Rutgers University in New Jersey to work on a doctorate in Byzantine history (which I finally received in 1972). In the fall of 1963 I began my college teaching career at Rhode Island College. At this point of my career I came to fully accept my gayness and to feel comfortable being gay. I began freely opening up to friends and close colleagues. However, I was wary of "coming out" publicly for fear of losing my job.

I left Rhode Island College in 1968 and in the fall of 1969 accepted a teaching position at West Georgia College, located fifty miles from Atlanta. Here I finally came out publicly in 1972. The occasion was the formation of a gay group on campus, to which I became the advisor. It was a very risky step for me to take since I had not as yet received tenure. My decision was facilitated by the support and solidarity I received from a newly-formed gay liberation group in Atlanta, which I had helped found.

Without their backing and support, I would not have gone public. Notwithstanding my openly gay stance at the college, I was given tenure in 1976.

Since I have come out, I have felt a tremendous burden lifted off my shoulders. I don't have to deceive when I talk about sexuality. I can openly talk about gay sexuality as it relates to life. Unfortunately, after all these years at West Georgia College, I still am the only openly gay professor on campus. But, at least I can be a role model for gay students at the college who are struggling with their sexual feelings. Moreover, periodically some of my colleagues in sociology and psychology invite me to speak to their classes on gay issues and the gay way of life.

My being gay has come up in the Orthodox church only in the parish I attend in Atlanta. There is a reason for this. Basically, I have made it a practice to come out only if the gay issue is brought up by others with whom I am associated. In 1983, the Archdiocesan monthly devoted several articles to homosexuality and the Orthodox faith, containing, I felt, a number of distortions. I wrote a letter to the editor. The author of one of the articles had advocated opening up a dialogue with gay Orthodox Christians. I prepared a rather lengthy piece stating that as a responsible gay Orthodox Christian I wished to begin dialogue within the Church on the gay issue. I went on to point out some of the distortions I felt I had discovered in the articles. The editor of the monthly turned my letter over to the bishop who, infuriated by its contents, himself sent a scathing letter attacking me to the priest at my parish. The priest then excommunicated me for six months until I finally agreed to retract my letter. What seemed to enrage the church hierarchy was that I dared to call myself gay and an Orthodox Christian at the same time. The support and encouragement of Integrity/Atlanta sustained me throughout these six trying months.

Individual Armenian friends have known of my sexual orientation for some time. I am certain that some other Armenians will be highly critical of my stance. However, I hope that many others will try to understand my viewpoint, and more than that, will learn to know and deal with those Armenians, young and old, who are going through experiences similar to mine. Moreover, I hope those Armenian youth at present struggling with their gay feelings will accept the validity of their sexual orientation and deal with it in a human, loving, and responsible way.

Many different ethnic, religious, social, and political groups have gay and lesbian organizations. I await the day when we Armenians can have our own gay and lesbian organization, committed to dispelling the fears and misunderstandings of many of our people, convincing those struggling gay and lesbian Armenians still in the closet that they are an integral part of the Armenian community and people.

Gary Ost's Story

At twelve I realized during a movie that the hero, not the heroine, turned me on. The ride home plunged me into the deepest depression I have ever experienced. It persisted until at fifteen I decided to become a minister. That decision gave me the feeling of self-worth I had lost. I vowed to myself and to God that I would never tell anyone that I harbored a desire that nobody could accept or even talk about.

Almost immediately I began to look for a steady girlfriend. Between the ages of 13 and 15, I went with three different girls. Then when my family moved, I set it up so that I had a girlfriend back in the other city. In that way I did not have to get serious with anyone in high school.

The decision isolated and frustrated me. I did not have any serious relationships. But I was so busy vying for first in my class that I put up with the stress.

Born in a suburb of Seattle, Washington, I have spent most of my life on the West Coast and most of that, except for some time in the city of Seattle, in suburban settings. I lived for the three years of high school in a suburb of Detroit. And for the last eight years I have lived in a suburb of San Francisco.

I was bent on attending either Michigan State or the University of Michigan, to both of which I had been awarded scholarships. I placed third in my graduating class of 500 and was voted "Most Likely To Succeed."

But I turned down the scholarships. My father retired from the Navy, my family decided to move back to

Seattle. Since my parents could not afford to support me financially through college, I was unwilling to let economic considerations separate me from my two younger brothers, especially my "baby brother," eleven years younger. I attended the University of Washington instead.

Proud German Russians, my family presented me for baptism in the Evangelical United Brethren Church, my maternal grandparents' church. Throughout childhood, my grandparents' piety influenced me more than did my parents' embarrassment about the strictness of their parents' religion. When the only church in the neighborhood was Southern Baptist, I thrived on the Sunday School there. My parents stayed at home.

At ten, I went with a friend to a Presbyterian Church, which attracted me with its sincere witness to a personal relationship with Christ. In time I led my parents in taking classes to join that church, and we were all confirmed together. I set my eyes on ministry in the Presbyterian Church when I was 15. I remained active in church throughout high school, although I moved back and forth between a Presbyterian Church and a Congregational Church which my parents preferred, because it reminded them of the country church they grew up in in North Dakota. So when I enrolled in college, I definitely had ordained ministry in mind. I immediately declared classical Greek as my major.

My first quarter I met Bev, an Episcopal co-ed, in Greek class. She was sincere and hospitable about sharing her religious experience. Since I was feeling parched spiritually, I became intrigued when she shared that she "spoke in tongues." After attending her church several times, I too had a "charismatic" experience, convinced both that I wanted to become a priest and to marry this woman.

I was confirmed in my sophomore year. Bev too had also been a loner. We were both bright, articulate, sincere, and pious. It felt right, so we married in my junior year, and we parented our first child (unexpectedly) in my senior year. From there we jumped immediately to seminary at the Church Divinity School of the Pacific in Berkeley, California. My daughter Liz was born in my second year of seminary.

Seminary was not the happiest of times. First, I was academically exhausted. I had become a serious student at the age of fifteen when I realized I had to work harder than my friends because of two things: I did not have rich parents, and I was not genius enough to "breeze through." I used to take books with me on school trips in high school, and I became expert at listing all the questions possible on an essay exam and memorizing exhaustive lists of points in response.

I longed to love and be loved in a way I had never experienced, and I fell in love with another seminarian. The feelings were too powerful to ignore. I tried to stuff them. I could not concentrate. I would lie on the couch staring at the ceiling. Tears would well up. I told Bev that I was experiencing a great block to studying. I thought I could not continue in seminary. Yet all my self-worth was tied up in becoming ordained. I felt trapped.

Finally I told Bev that I had fallen in love with a man. At first she felt relief. At least I was not having an affair with another woman. Then she felt curious, and set out to learn everything she could about homosexuality.

I shored up my seminary education. After four incompletes in my middler year, I took a secular job for the summer and had time to think. I recovered energy for my senior year.

Two weeks after commencement I drove my young family back to Tacoma, for my first parish assignment, as a deacon. Six months later the bishop invited me to take a mission on my own.

So at 26, I began my career as a country priest in a beautiful retirement community on the north Olympic Peninsula. I had a bright career going for me. My parish was growing. I was gaining respect both as a youth leader and as a lecturer. I had two beautiful children and a wife who was as eager for ministry as I was.

In fact, in some ways, Bev was a little too eager--for me. She began to respond to an ancient urging of her own. Since childhood she had felt strangely drawn to the altar. Only none of the traditional avenues open for women satisfied the longing. As the Church began to open doors for women, she felt more and more called to pursue ordination. The threat for me was not that she would upstage me (though we have always had a healthy rivalry), nor that she would require me to stick my neck out for an as-yet-unpopular cause. The threat was that she was taking the opportunity to answer the urges in her life, and I could not do the same!

My loneliness for a man's love had not diminished. I did not do anything about my feelings for that seminarian except tell him how I felt toward him. Now four years into my ministry, my longings reasserted themselves. At first I dealt with them by getting into therapy with a psychologist. Then I became distracted by pursuing a position as rector of a large suburban Seattle parish. I got the position at 30.

Inevitably I met a man, a handsome care-giver by profession. He said he had fallen in love, too. After struggling briefly, I reciprocated. I put my marriage and my career on the auction block and seriously considered leaving all for him. Bev and I separated, and I resigned as rector.

But I was not sure. I was still involved in charismatic renewal. I wondered whether I was wrong. Maybe the chaos in my life derived from sickness?

I left for a personal pilgrimage to a center I had read about in southern California. They were considered a successful "exodus" ministry for people to leave behind their homosexuality. If I could avoid the destruction I saw facing my life, I was willing to give up Don. I visited the center.

The director of this ministry was himself gay and now felt that the Center itself wrongly forced people to suppress their feelings. When a male client reported he had withstood temptation to look at a man, the Center cheered. But the director confided in me that he was planning to leave as soon as he got a master's and could start counseling on his own. I told him about Don.

"Do you love him?" the director asked. I was amazed.

"Yes."

"What is so wrong with that?"

Going home I made a side trip to my parents' winter place in Arizona. I knew that my mother was hurt by my confession by letter that I am a homosexual, but I did not know how my father felt. He has never been very communicative. On the bus I thought about my life. I had left a wife and two children whom I loved very much, although my emotions for my wife were blocked at the time. I had left the greatest source of self-esteem in my life, my position as a parish priest. I had no job waiting for me. Now I did not know whether my parents still loved me. I wondered whether my father would greet my face with his fist. Did I have courage for all this? Had I blown God's trust, ignored the tender moments on several occasions when I felt called by God? Did God still love me?

I stared out the window at a sky of broken alto-cumulus clouds. Suddenly I felt as though I stood on a pavement before God in heaven. I felt as though God asked: "Gary, will you do something for Me?"

What startled me was not so much the question, but the words which formed immediately in my head: "But you 're the Lord, Lord. There's no question. I'm the servant. You're the master. My life is dedicated to you. But what about Don?"

I needed to know if I was outside of God's will.

"I am Love," God answered.

How like the Transcendent to speak ambiguously. Did God mean, "Love is love; love for a man is just as holy as love for a woman." Or did God mean, "I am the standard for all love. You can love Don while doing the sacrificially loving thing: Go back to your wife."

I am convinced that God cares less about the issue of homosexuality than people do; God cares immensely about individuals genuinely working out the appropriate expression of their love.

Still afraid to "ruin" four lives, I gave "healing" one more try, this time with a psychotherapist. After a year and the additional motivation of Don's return to his wife, I returned to Bev. I see now that part of my attraction was to the idea of leaving Seattle and starting afresh in California, since Bev had transferred her credits to C.D.S.P. I had a good job as a manager in the Bell System, so I was able to transfer easily, and I looked forward to supporting her without the hassles of parish responsibilities myself.

We thought we could make it. But we couldn't.

One year later, deadness returned to our affection. I felt I was dying emotionally. When Bev returned from a weekend away, on the way home from the airport we found ourselves saying, almost simultaneously, "You know, I really did not miss you this weekend."

We began the painful ending of our marriage. A year later it was complete. We separated kindly. We scored a first in California by crossing out the words, "petitioner" and "defendant" and writing in "co-petitioner." It was a no-fault divorce, using the same attorney and seeing the same divorce counselor for the emotional issues. Our child support agreement has worked well, and we have remained friends. My son continued living with me till he graduated from high school. Liz lived with both of us for two years before it was apparent she needed more time with her mother. They have lived together for Liz's last two years of high school in northern Minnesota, where Bev has a parish of her own.

The first two years after my divorce, I just enjoyed being true to myself. I had gone back into parochial ministry only a year before, and the people at St. Luke's took the news well. I remember being happy just coming home to do domestic chores. However, I also had much growing to do regarding being alone. I had never had to confront aloneness. I tried desperately to make relationships with a few men. None of them really worked, although I learned a lot.

I decided to go about meeting new people in another way. I had gone with a friend to a Western gay dance bar in San Francisco. The people there looked like they were just having fun. Friendships were happening. There were free dance lessons in the evening. I took myself to my first night of lessons. I had just chosen a partner for the evening when a young-looking man walked into the room and stood in the corner. I did a double-take, struck mostly by his youth. But I had come to learn to dance, so I ignored the temptation to look again. Later that evening, after the lesson, the young man asked me for a dance. That dance would begin one of the most beautiful chapters of my life.

Ken was, in fact, a few months older than I. We had many values in common, including Church of the Brethren backgrounds. Plus, he was committed to a life of service, as a doctor. After dating six months, I knew this was the man I wanted to spend my life with. I told my parents so. My children met him and liked him.

Since we lived 60 miles apart, we took turns commuting. It wasn't so bad, really, since our professions kept us so busy in between. We were together at least three nights of the week, including most weekends. We enjoyed dancing together. We enjoyed music together. He introduced me to opera. He gave me ski lessons. We looked at the possibility of buying an apartment together in San Francisco, just for the weekends. How wonderfully indulgent! But Ken developed a cough nine months after we met. It was a harbinger.

We could not get a firm diagnosis. Even a bronchoscopy revealed nothing. One Saturday, I decided to surprise Ken by meeting him at the airport as he returned from a medical conference. He almost crawled off the plane and gasped, "Get me a wheelchair." By the following Monday he was in the hospital with pneumocystis AIDS. A battle for love was about to begin.

I thought Ken was getting better. But when I returned from work one evening, he was not in his room. Panicked, I asked where he was. They told me he had been moved to intensive care. Even then I did not know how serious things were. But his doctor came and told me plainly, "You guys have to make a decision immediately. If you do not put him on a respirator, he probably will not make it through the night."

Till then, Ken had shown signs of caving in, accepting the inevitability of his diagnosis as only a doctor can. But I turned to him and said, "Ken, whatever you want to do, I'll back you. Only, just tell me--do you want more time?" He thought about it only a second and answered, "Yes."

With that I asked, "May I please call your parents?" He said yes. I knew I would have called them even if he had said no. The technicians raced to bring equipment into his room. Within the hour he was on a respirator and by morning his parents arrived from Virginia.

I fought to give Ken as much quality of life as I could, and we went for as much quantity as God would allow. I prayed for two things at once--that God would help me let go of him and just love him unconditionally and that God would heal him miraculously. I felt God gave me a verse of scripture to cling to: "Have I not told you, that if you would believe you would see the glory of God?" I was ready for the glory to be either the vision of eternity with God or a medical first in the war against AIDS--and I told Ken so.

After five weeks on the respirator, from which he was not expected to recover, we walked him out of the hospital to begin the long convalescence at home. Due largely to my efforts, he was put on AZT soon thereafter and pentamidine mist treatments, both of which were still experimental. Two months later he was walking outside for the first time. Two months after that his parents drove him to my house for his birthday party. Two months after that we went for an outing alone up the north coast of California and then he traveled with his parents to Virginia for Christmas and returned by car! But the most miraculous thing of all: two months after that, he and I kept our date with a group of friends to ski in Aspen for a whole week. He looked marvelous and I was so happy.

But the disease was insidious. I knew he was worried. Two months later, the cough worsened. I suspected a return of pneumocystis. He increased the frequency of pentamidine treatments. But he pushed himself to go to Alaska with his parents, a trip they had long dreamed of. When he returned, he looked weaker than before he left. But he was strong enough to pull off a surprise birthday party for me. Then he put me on a plane to Detroit because he wanted me to keep my commitment to help out with the Integrity presence at General Convention.

I called him every day from Convention. At times it sounded like his voice was stronger. I persuaded myself his treatments were working. But when I saw him, I was frightened by his shuffle. He was dragging more in energy. Yet the doctor said the pneumocystis had cleared up. What was going on? Two weeks later it became clear. He blacked out on the way to the bathroom. When he came to, he looked up into my eyes and said, "I had so hoped to spare you all this."

I had conveniently forgotten that a year earlier x-rays had shown lesions on his brain. I thought the AZT had forever taken care of those. As a radiologist, Ken knew better. I began to say goodbye.

At once the comatose episodes increased in frequency and in length. Pressure built in his cranium. I began my vigil, along with his parents, his brother, his sister, and our close friends. I gave him last rites and read poetry to him all night long the night before he died. Earlier that afternoon he had spoken to me for the last time. When I arrived, he awoke from his coma. I said, "Remember, I love you," code words which both of us had used for the last year and a half to prepare for just this. He looked at me and said, "I know," or "I love you, too--" I can't remember which. He died at 8:20 on the evening of July 30th, 1988.

I loved him very much.

In preparing his memorial service, I made a fateful decision. With the encouragement of the two employees I talked to at the *San Francisco Chronicle*, I included "and survived by his lover, Gary W. D. Ost." I did not intend to "come out." I responded to my grief and I re sponded to the encouragement I felt I had received from my bishop. On a couple of occasions he had let gay couples show themselves in the authenticity of their relationships as a witness to the Church for the appropriateness of blessing their unions. People naturally and authentically memorialize love by acknowledging it in a funeral notice. Since I felt Ken and I were as close as any married people--or at least engaged people, since our relationship was still young, I felt I was doing only what was appropriate.

People did read it and started talking. Before long, my wardens asked me to come out to my vestry so we could decide whether we could continue doing ministry together. After three negotiating sessions with the executive officer of the diocese, we have decided we can live with each other for at least the next eight months. My letter of agreement was renewed until June 30, 1989, at which time we will decide whether we should dissolve the relationship and seek terms of departure.

I think the Church needs someone to stay put after he or she has come out of the closet about sexual orientation and show to the world that people somewhere can make it work. I think my people love me and appreciate my ministry. I love them, too, so we might even be able to make it work here.

I cannot shake my conviction that the time may have come for me to take the next step toward fulfilling the call God gave me on that bus on the way to Arizona.